All Scripture is from
the New Living Translation.

Most of the names in this work
have been changed to protect
the privacy of the
individuals involved.

We all struggle to believe a better story through the noise and confusion of our inner worlds and past experiences. Wilkinson weaves an honest expose of humanity's entrapment in a mortal cage- often of our own making. This is a vulnerable and scholarly journey across ethnic, gender and faith community boundaries toward hope, life and love. Readers will be stretched at many points to think and believe differently about the story they may now embrace. Well worth the read.

Jack A. Taylor (Ph.D.) — Author of 8 novels, including the award-winning series *The Cross Maker trilogy* and *The One Last Wave trilogy.*

This book does not have all the answers. It offers so much more. Through his personal experiences, Wilkinson exemplifies how to navigate the path of faith with unwavering honesty, curiosity, thoughtfulness, and compassion. Rather than relying on shallow responses and tired clichés, he fearlessly explores the pivotal questions and topics that can hinder one's faith if left unaddressed. I wholeheartedly recommend this book to anyone drawn to Christianity, including those who approach it with caution or hostility. It will captivate readers from all walks of life. Personally, I wish I had had this book when I first embarked on my journey of faith. I'm grateful to have it now.

Alastair Sterne — Creative director turned pastor and writer. Author of *Rhythms for Life: Spiritual Practices For Who God Made You To Be.* He holds degrees from The Art Institute, Asbury Theological Seminary, and a Doctorate in Intercultural Studies from Fuller Theological Seminary.

The Romans had a term for it: Quo Vadis? For those embraced by their shackles instead of their dreams, this book is for you. Christian and non-believer alike will find something here to contemplate, consider, and perhaps even argue with. An excellent meditation on life's Q&A. A very entertaining read!

Randolph Eustace-Walden — Author of *Aloha Wanderwell: The Border-smashing, Record-setting Life of the World's Youngest Explorer* and Television Producer.

A raw, honest, personal, revealing journey about real concerns we all have on our spiritual journey. Elegantly written with compelling stories heard by a pastor diligently trying to follow his calling.

Larry Nelson — Senior Advisor, Nelson/Kraft & Associates Inc.

What an inspiring and insightful look at the culture we're living in and witnessing. In this very personal account of Wilkinson's journey, you will see the world through different lenses. The book is full of fascinating and engaging stories that get you thinking and cause you to evaluate your presuppositions.

Ron Leonard — Canadian Director of the C2C Collective.

The stories in this book share so much in common with the author - always personable, usually intense, sometimes startling, never submissive to easy moralizing. Wilkinson writes earworm stories that tunnel into your brain and (I think) open pathways for the Spirit's light to shine in. This book holds no mystical or magical key for unlocking your mortal cage; but beware: it is a sturdy crowbar that just might bend apart some of your cage's stoutest and most stubborn bars.

Tim Kuepfer — English congregation pastor, Chinatown Peace Church.

Whether you are facing doubts, not wanting to face them, or desiring to help others face theirs, you will appreciate this book. Wilkinson writes with raw honesty and compelling stories. He raises important questions, and though it's an easy read, he doesn't give easy answers - that isn't the point. Amidst the confusing questions of life, love, and God, there is hope and beauty that is worth reaching for. Wilkinson has lived in the tensions and continues to persevere in faith. This book will help others do the same.

Brett Donald — Founder and Visionary Equipper, CityLights Church. Adjunct Instructor, Pacific Life Bible College.

God has given us no easy answers to the reality of suffering. And in the Mortal Cage, Dennis does not provide any. But he charts a path with story and wisdom that sits alongside suffering and doubt, and shows us how to run the race well.

Christopher Mark — President of Vintality Tech Inc. & Speaker.

For Grandpa Arve, whose name I happily share and whose faith-filled life set the right example.

For my indomitable mother, who has weathered so many storms and still manages to squeeze out the joy.

For my wife, Mistin. I love you. You are my best friend. Your one-of-a-kind name fits your one-of-a-kind personality. You are the perfect blend of passion, care, strength, ferocity and joy. I am fortunate beyond what words can properly express to have you in my life.

And finally, for the four sprigs that have sprouted from our union: Ciara, Tikki, Darve, and Jemma, I am proud of you all. It is my hope that, something in this book will help you as you chart your way in this uncertain world.

The Mortal Cage

Bounded to this temporal world

Stuck fast in material existence

Our age disagrees with thoughts of more

All we need is here and now

Let the ancient stories be forgotten.

The air is thick with the scent of our insignificance

But the loss is merely the price of growing up

We chart our path — the world is what we make it

All we need is here and now

Human! Settle into your mortal cage.

The verdict is in; the world is closed. Get used to it.

Mortal: One who cannot live forever.
Cage: A structure meant for confining.

I found myself stuck in a mortal cage. I was increasingly convinced that the material world is all that exists and that death is the end. I didn't like this conclusion. I felt entrapped by it, suffocated by it; but I despaired of finding a way out. It wasn't always like this. From birth, I had lived under the assumption that humans were immortal. Within this worldview, I embraced heaven; hell; God; eternity; grand, overarching purposes; deeper meanings; spiritual realities; an unseen world; divine interventions in human history; and hope beyond the grave. In my youth, these were obvious truths, "no brainers" drummed into my mind and heart through believing parents plus countless Sunday school classes and church services. But then life happened, and all my assumptions were sorely challenged. This book is the story of my descent into the mortal cage and my slow, improbable, and still struggling escape from it.

If you, like me, are full of doubts and have come to suspect or even believe fully that the mortal cage is all there is, perhaps as you resonate with my entrapment and then trace the steps of my escape, you will find an escape of your own. Dear reader, this is my hope for you; a cage, after all, is no place to live.

In Part One, I will share my downward progression into the cage. I'm hoping my honest struggle, as it nakedly appears in print, will not bind you further. If you find that you are agreeing with my skepticism and despair too much, please keep reading! In Part Two, I will share ten discoveries I found along the way that have helped me, however imperfectly, bend the bars of my imprisonment and escape the mortal cage. Part Two is the heartbeat of this book.

These breakthroughs have helped me the most by far. However, for those that have picked up my book hoping to find a more robust defence of the faith, you won't be completely disappointed if you can manage to make it to Part Three. In this section, I will shift from a focus on matters of the heart as they relate to belief to more traditional arguments defending the faith. In 23 years of professional ministry, I heard these objections to Christianity over and over again; consequently, I became pretty good at having an answer.

Contents

Part One — Trapped

Chapter 1 – **Greeks, lesbians, and church planting:**
A recipe for doubt 23

Chapter 2 – **Pain in Palestine:**
All religions are well-meaning but corrupt 31

Chapter 3 – **Surviving Sarajevo:** Divine love? Nonsense.
Human survival is the truth 39

Chapter 4 – **Insanity in Iraq:**
All that matters is being a good person 43

Chapter 5 – **Madness in the Middle East:**
If God is dead, he must surely have died
trying to fix the Jewish-Arab problem 51

Chapter 6 – **Sex:** Christianity's achilles' heel 59

Part Two — Escape

Chapter 7 — **Some help from the doubters** 77

Chapter 8 — **Faith is what drives us all** 85

Chapter 9 — **To be human is to have a story** 93

Chapter 10 — **Some stories are better than others. One in particular rises above all the rest** 99

Chapter 11 — **Most stories in the West are poached versions of the Christian one** 113

Chapter 12 — **What does your heart long for? Listen to that** 119

Chapter 13 — **Certainty is overrated** 137

Chapter 14 — **Modern apologetics: An adventure in missing the point** 145

Chapter 15 — **Overcoming Biblical Attachment Disorder (B.A.D.)** 155

Chapter 16 — **The power of a changed life** 167

Part Three — Yeah, but what about...

Chapter 17 — **Do life's brutality and the absence of God ruin the better story?** 181

Chapter 18 — **Does the Bible's support of slavery ruin the better story?** 189

Chapter 19 — **Do the Bible's sexist perspectives ruin the better story?** 199

Chapter 20 — **Does the Bible's support of genocide ruin the better story?** 211

Chapter 21 — **Does the Bible's support of hell ruin the better story?** 221

Chapter 22 — **Do the Bible's prudish views on sex ruin the better story?** 235

Conclusion: Escaping the Mortal Cage 251

Part One
Trapped

Alas, how easily things go wrong!
A sigh too much, a kiss too long and
here follows a mist and a weeping rain.
And life is never the same again.
George MacDonald

My natural tendency is to move in a direction away from the supernatural. Why? Perhaps the main reason is my observation of life itself. All too often, my hope for more is obscured by the misery of life on earth and a perceived absence of God in the middle of it all. I want to lift my eyes to the heavens, but when I do, I see only the sky.

Chapter 1

Greeks, lesbians, and church planting: A recipe for doubt

I was in my mid-twenties on an airplane headed to Athens. Thrilled to be going on a study tour of Greece and Italy, I plastered my face against the window as we approached this great city. So much history waited for me down below. As a young Christian, I was excited to think that the great Apostle Paul had walked these streets. The older gentleman next to me was not as enthusiastic. He was engrossed in his newspaper, and only a wild shock of white hair protruded above it. He did not even peek up from his paper as the plane banked to reveal a spectacular view of the old city. I tried to pick out the Acropolis, where Paul on nearby Mars Hill would have given his famous sermon about the Unknown God to the intellectuals of his day. I was trying to imagine it all when my thoughts were interrupted; the man with the wild hair had folded his newspaper and was looking at me. With a thick Greek accent, he asked me why I was coming to his country. I happily told him about my faith and this great opportunity I had to study the Bible in the context of its actual geography. He was pleasant and asked a few more questions as the plane landed. When the seat belt sign dinged off, we unbuckled and began gathering our things. Just as we got up to exit, he tilted his head slightly to look over the top of his spectacles directly into my eyes. He said, "Since you are a Christian, you should know that we have rid our country of that disease."

He smiled, bowed slightly, and was gone. He wanted me to put my Christianity away before it hurt someone! I was stunned and left to wonder what was so bad about my Christian faith that it ranks up there with the bubonic plague. I didn't get a chance to ask him. His laconic summation of the value of my belief system took the wind out of my sails.

The man's words stuck with me, eating at me. If I was honest with myself, I too had doubts and struggles with my faith in quiet moments. It bugged me that I couldn't put my misgivings to bed. So I read and researched. I studied and went to seminary, but the more I worked at bolstering my faith, the more trapped by doubt I seemed to become. In my first decade of pastoral ministry, I managed well enough. Perhaps it helped that I was insulated: I was a Christian minister, working with beautiful people in a Christian bubble. There weren't too many Grecian zealots wandering around my neighbourhood trying to knock me off my spiritual game.

Then my neighbourhood changed. In 2010, 13 years after my time in Athens, my wife, Mistin, and I with our four small kids moved nearly 3,000 kilometres away from our Christian bubble in Minnesota to Vancouver, Canada. The plan was to move into a neighbourhood that had very little Christian influence connected to it. The strategy was to be present, available, and helpful to anyone in that neighbourhood. The goal was to see what incredible works of transformation God might do as the good news of Jesus slowly spread through intentional community-oriented living.

It didn't take long to realize what I might be up against.

"You are white, male, straight, and Christian; what the hell are you doing in my neighbourhood?"

The question came just a few months after we made the big move. It came from our new neighbor, Sarah, a lesbian who lived nearby with her two children. Of these four strikes against my existence, I got the distinct impression that the most intolerable aspect of my being was my Christianity.

I had no idea how to answer this question, so I didn't; instead I invited her to join us for a BBQ. Vancouver's West End is a gorgeous neighbourhood tucked in on all sides by picturesque marinas, beaches, and parks. With traffic-calmed streets and beautiful overhanging trees, the West End is a prized location. It is also the centre of an activist culture led by a vocal and powerful LGBTQ+ community, hence the question.

We eventually befriended Sarah and her children, and thankfully we moved beyond this icy beginning. We spent six years with her before cancer snuffed out her life. She even flirted with becoming a follower of Jesus.

After a year or two in our neighbourhood, our relationship with Sarah and many of her friends had progressed to the degree that we felt good about inviting them over to our house for something we called food and philosophy. We gathered together for wine and cheese and Mistin's famous wontons, enjoying a laughter-filled evening. Finally, once the noise began to die down, I motioned for everyone's attention and all eyes focused on me. Smiling, I confessed that my philosophy of life came from someone named Jesus, whose words were found in a holy book known as the Bible. People set their cheese down and stopped sipping their wine at this point. I had everyone's attention now!

Then I asked: "Does anyone else follow Jesus or believe the Bible?"

A disapproving murmur rippled through the crowd as arms began to fold and eyebrows arched in disapproval. After a few seconds of uncomfortable silence, the room erupted in one giant collective refutation.

"Hell, no!"

"Can you tell me why?" I asked. For the next 90 minutes, I scribbled furiously, writing down one objection after another.

- The story of God must be false because evolution is true.

- Christianity is a bad idea because it exists solely as a tool for control.

- The Bible reinforces unhealthy habits of sexual repression.

- The presence of miracles in the Bible invalidates any truth that might come from it.

- Nothing can be proven or known conclusively about many ancient Biblical characters. How can we believe that what they said or say they saw is true?

- The Bible promotes slavery, which is wrong.

- The Bible treats women as inferior, which is wrong.

- The Bible is homophobic, which is wrong.

- Biblical truth is all about interpretation anyway; since there are so many interpretations, we must conclude that if there is divine truth found in the Bible we can never actually know it for certain.

- The Bible embraces eternal judgment. The idea of a fiery torture chamber that goes on forever is utterly deplorable!

- The bloody faith, as described in the Bible, is barbaric, not beautiful.

- We don't think about sin the way the Bible does anymore.

- Any God who mandates genocide is not a God worth worshiping.

- The exclusive claims that salvation is found only in Jesus are far too narrow for our pluralistic world.

- The undisputed corruption of the church supports the idea that the Bible must itself be corrupt.

In a single night, all of my doubts and misgivings were shoved in my face. At first, I felt somewhat excited to rebut all these objections. But over time, I began to feel more like I was bailing water on a sinking boat.

For the next ten years, my family and I lived in this neighbourhood, running a small but enthusiastic community church that accomplished a lot of good. I put up an admirable fight tirelessly defending the faith with all of the best rational and evidential argumentation I could muster. As the years passed, I became a bit of an expert at dredging up clever answers for skeptics. I read one apologetic book after another to have a ready answer for every doubt lobbed in my direction. But over time I became weary. I was battling against something that started to feel inevitable. The story of "this is all there is," the story that my neighbours felt so confident about, seemed irresistible to me. Like the Borg from Star Trek, this competing story spoke with such certainty: "Resistance is futile; you will be assimilated, and your life as it has been is over."

The Greek on the plane, the lesbian who "welcomed" me to her neighbourhood, and all the friends who filled up my living room that night were unable to see the beauty of God's love because of an unceasing flow of doubts, objections, and "deal breakers." At some point along my journey, I poked my head up from all the defending I had been doing and found that I could no longer "stand up for Jesus" with the passion or conviction I once had. If I was honest, I shared the same problems they had with my faith system. Adding to all this internal angst was an experiential lack. For all my talk of God, my experience of him in any tangible sense was largely absent.

Attacks on our community from outside activists and internal divisions with other Christians compounded the crushing weight of self-doubt and ministry weariness. I felt as though I was being squashed. I looked to the Bible for solace, as I had so many times before, but this time instead of relief and buoyed faith, there came confusion and even more doubt.

I reached for God in prayer, but the more I called out to God, the less I sensed him. I cleared my mornings to sit quietly in nature to try to listen for any sign of his presence. The effort proved fruitless. That niggling feeling in the back of my neck activated itself more than ever. Maybe I've been wrong all these years, I thought. Maybe there is nothing to hope in outside of humanity and the here and now. The weight of it all pressed down hard, and slowly but surely the breath of faith squeezed out of me. I looked around, and for the first time all I could see were bars.

Chapter 2

Pain in Palestine:
All religions are well-meaning but corrupt

I saw him through the coffee shop window. He was alone, so I decided to pop in and say hi. I had seen him around a few times, and he had even helped out at one of our community-building events, so I thought I would try turning an acquaintance into a friend.

I entered the shop and greeted him with a big smile and a handshake. It wasn't long before I asked him, "Where are you from?" I immediately noticed discomfort in his demeanour. He hesitated on the answer, shifting uneasily. Finally, he told me he was from Jerusalem, followed by a mumble that he was Palestinian. To make an awkward situation even worse, I foolishly asked an even more insensitive question: "Oh, so do you hate Jews?"

In the grand universe of possible questions to ask, why would I ever ask that one? I was getting full marks for callous, dunderheaded stupidity that day! Upon reflection, I realized why I had asked the question. The night before, I had watched the short documentary We Refuse To Be Enemies, about the Christian Palestinian family of Amal Nassar. For generations, the Nassar family owned and operated a beautiful family farm on a hilltop in the West Bank. After the 1967 war, Israel slowly began to siphon off the natural resources surrounding the family farm, then eventually began to expand five Jewish settlements across the Nassar property lines. In 1991, the entire farm was declared "state land." The Nassar family refused to take the hint from the Israeli government; moving away was inconceivable to them. Finally, in 2014, after decades of methodical encroachment, the Israeli government bulldozed 1,500 of their fruit trees. Understandably they were frustrated, but when the matriarch of the family was interviewed for the documentary, she said, "As Christians, we don't want to repay evil with evil, but instead evil with good. We will plant new trees and ask God to give us the strength to get up again. We have to follow in the footsteps of Christ; we have to love our enemy. We use three strategies as we struggle to hang on to our land: faith, hope, and love."

This heroic family genuinely believes that the overarching story of Jesus mandates that their lives be filled with faith, hope, and love, not violence, revenge, and hate. They willingly let the story shape their lives even amid injustice and suffering because they believe it is ultimately a better story. This does not mean they are not attempting to get justice for themselves. They were willing to do the documentary; perhaps by letting the world know about their plight, public pressure could create a different outcome than what seems inevitable. Regardless, whatever happens, the

Nassars cling to their hope in Jesus more than their hope in retaining their land. The documentary finished with a shot of a large stone erected on what little of the family's property remains. In several languages etched on the rock are the words, "We refuse to be enemies."

In a bull-in-a-China-shop way, I was fishing around to see if this man might be anchored to the same story as this amazing Palestinian family.

His eyes got big. In a controlled voice, he told me: "I don't hate Jewish people, I try not to hate anybody. But I have a real problem with Zionists."

I understood. The struggle not to hate a group of people that is actively against your own is very, very real. I immediately apologized for my insensitivity and told him all about the video I had just watched. At this point, he offered to buy me coffee. By some miracle, the conversation wasn't destroyed by my stupidity.

Not long into the conversation, he asked me if I wanted to know why he came to Canada.

"Sure," I said.

"I am running from God. Religion in the Middle East is all fucked up!" he told me. He also let me know that as far as he is concerned, all the religions in the world are the same.

I asked him what his religious heritage was. He responded with the blunt question; "Does it matter? It doesn't to me. All religions are the same. They all mean well initially, but then they are hijacked and perverted by power-hungry opportunists, and God is silent."

Since I had already put my foot in my mouth too many times in our short conversation, I decided to listen instead of talk.

He told me that he appreciated our community-building efforts in the neighbourhood, but if they ever smelled religious to him, he would run in the other direction. Eventually, the conversation drifted back to the sad story of his people.

"Palestinians have always been here. We were here before the Jews, the Christians, and the Muslims. We became Jews, Christians, and Muslims, but we are the people who were here first; and to have Russians, Poles, and Romanians coming back to our homeland masquerading as Jews and destroying us is just wrong. I am more Jewish than any of those people coming back as Zionists!

"Just like the people in your story my father and grandfather refuse to leave, which will eventually cost them everything. The Jews have all the power right now, but they won't always. It makes sense for them to make peace with us when we are weak because if they don't, when we are strong; all the suffering they've put us through will be returned to them."

He paused. "Tell me, Dennis: how is it that a God could pick one people group over another? How could God ask them to kill off others? Something is wrong with God if this is true."

I shook my head sadly and said, "For dark reasons, humans of all kinds have had this propensity for killing each other en masse."

I had just finished the book *The Fall of the Ottomans*, which describes the Armenian and Palestinian genocides, both perpetrated by the Turks during World War One. We talked about all the suffering that has gone on, and together we acknowledged that much of the world is not the way it should be.

I wanted to believe that all our mutual angst and frustration against this darkness must be evidence that there is divine light. I wanted to share this thought with my friend; but the words and, more importantly, the faith behind them wasn't there. I offered weakly, "Conversations of morality don't get easier if God is pushed out of the picture."

My friend put his coffee cup down and looked straight into my eyes. "I am not an anti-God person," he said. "I am just a confused and discouraged person. It's all just a mess. Where is God?"

I had no answers for him.

It was time for us to go pick up our children from school. As we walked past the playground, he looked at the children laughing and playing, and said: "See all these children? Why would we divide them up into Jews and Christians and Muslims, and somehow make them worth more or less based on these divisions?"

"We sure shouldn't," is all I could say.

Our time together was finished. I apologized once more for the uncharitable way I had entered into our conversation. He assured me that it was okay. Later that night, I sent him the link to the video about the Palestinian family. In the email, I told him: "I think their attitude is beautiful, just like Jesus—but their situation is so sad."

To my friend, the Christian story is just one of many good stories eventually corrupted by power, and God does nothing to intervene. If God is involved at all, he's managed to make things worse by setting apart a people group and blessing them at the expense of other people groups, to such a degree that, in the Old Testament, brutal violence is justified against the ones who are not "God's Chosen." Today, with the backing of pro-Israel American evangelicals, the violence continues. Israel is "God's Chosen," after all. Perhaps it is a good story if you are Jewish, but not if you happen to be in their way.

That day, I felt wholly inadequate to speak hope into this man; in many respects, I still do. I know nothing of the difficulties he has faced, and while the Nassars are a shining example of one Palestinian family doggedly clinging to Jesus' way of peace and non-violence, it is easy to see why they are the dramatic exception to the rule. It is also a challenge to see how their stance is the right one. Eventually they too will be forced out, whether they fight or not. They will be crushed.

My Palestinian friend cannot grasp faith in the better story of divine love, and his circumstance also makes it more difficult for me to grasp. He can only despair as humans divide themselves into religious and political factions and then destroy each other in a never-ending struggle for land, power, and control. As far as God is concerned, my friend can't hear him. Any sound of divine love is drowned out by the roar of bulldozers doing their work.

Chapter 3

Surviving Sarajevo:
Divine love? Nonsense.
Human survival is the truth

She was from a mixed family, one parent Christian and the other Muslim; they lived in Sarajevo at precisely the wrong time. Things looked grim when the Serbs took to the hills and besieged her city. It was no longer safe to walk the streets—snipers saw to that. It was no longer safe to hide at home—artillery barrages and tanks saw to that. As supplies dwindled and the situation became more desperate, she and her neighbours had to begin seriously considering risky escape plans.

An artillery blast killed Natasha's father. Another reduced her brother to a vegetative state. It was time to go. She and her remaining family secured the bribe money and hired a sympathetic Serb to run the blockade around the city. In the middle of the night my friend and a few others made their move. At first, the daring escape appeared successful, but sadly escape plans were thwarted when a roving band of Serb militia captured her the next day. They locked her in a makeshift prison, which had previously been a village school. Natasha is beautiful, a feature the predatory jailers did not fail to notice and exploit for their benefit. She did what she had to do to survive, but her prospects of making it out alive had become very bleak.

For centuries Croats, Muslims, and Serbs had lived together in relative peace in the Balkans. This meant the war often turned former schoolmates and best friends into enemy combatants, making the carnage from the ethnic conflicts of the 1990s all the more difficult to comprehend. One day a former classmate of my friend, who was fighting for the Serbian side, walked into the prison. As he passed through, he recognized her. In a quiet moment he whispered that the prison was to be burned and all inside with it. He gave her a pair of scissors and told her to cut her hair and wait for his return that night. All she could do was obey and try to suppress the panic welling up inside.

Natasha's life had come down to a single hope in a saviour who said he would come. He did come, bringing a Serbian military uniform with him. A quick change, a few bribes and back doorways, and they were off. When they reached relative safety he bid her farewell. She never looked back. Her journey to freedom was arduous, but eventually she landed in Canada.

When Natasha told me her story I called her a superhero. She rejected the title, preferring to be called a survivor. We find in her incredible story a saviour staging a daring rescue that saves her from suffering and death. The heart of Christianity contains this same hope in a saviour, a person who will deliver us from our own suffering and death. The best stories have a constant thread of hope running through them just like this: hope that culminates in some glorious way, not by our own doing but by the doing of one who has wished to help us. However, my friend is unable to see God's story in her own. Life has taught her to keep people at arm's length. Survival depends upon partnerships, deals and trusting nobody but oneself.

Natasha had to become strong or die. She survived, but it was she who made it happen. God didn't offer divine help to my friend. What about divine love? Nonsense. Survival is her story. She did whatever it took to make a life for herself. In her experience, those who wait for the help of invisible friends die. This is her reality; it's her story. She cannot see the thread of God's good providence that others might recognize in bringing her through all the trauma. The bodies of the unfortunate ones that fill the ditches on both sides of her fortuitous trail make sure of that.

For everyone like my friend who made it thousands more did not. Because of this, transcendent visions that shape how we understand reality are almost offensive to her. She survived, and that is enough. She does not want to be considered blessed by God while so many others rot in shallow graves across her shattered former country. Natasha has today to live, today to figure out how to keep living. It is a mortal cage, but for her it has to be enough.

Chapter 4

Insanity in Iraq:
All that matters is being a good person

His father's fist crashed down upon his head. He crumpled in pain.

"Don't ever ask such questions again! If someone other than me heard you say what you just said, it would be much worse for you than my hand across your face!" His father's words hit as hard as his fists.

My friend Ishmael was only twelve or thirteen. When he managed to read somewhere that the prophet Mohammed had married an eight-year-old, he was disgusted that anyone would do such a thing, let alone the holy prophet. He spoke up, but he quickly learned that accusing the prophet of sin was intolerable blasphemy in the Kurdish culture of Northern Iraq. The beating my friend got from his father was a light punishment for such sacrilege. My friend learned to control his disgust and keep his mouth shut.

Being Kurdish in Iraq during the reign of Saddam Hussein was hardly idyllic, especially if, like Ishmael, you had family members who were part of the nationalist Peshmerga group. The plight of the Kurds for generations has hovered somewhere between bleak and tragic. A long-standing joke my friend shared with me about the impossibility of the Kurdish situation captures the challenges before his people:

> One day three people went to visit God. One was an American, the other a Japanese, and the third a Kurd. The American asked God, "When are we going to be able to control the whole world?" God thought for a moment, then said, "It's possible. It could happen but it will take 200 years." The American cried and walked away. "Why did you cry?" God asked. "I will not live to see it," replied the American. The Japanese person stepped forward and asked, "When are we going to control the world with our technology?" God said "It's possible, it could happen, but it will take 300 years." The Japanese person, like the American, cried and walked away. Finally, the Kurd stepped forward to ask God his question: "When are we going to be able to get our own country?" God cried and walked away.

The problem of Kurdish sovereignty is "a hole that's bigger than the dress," says my friend. But the Peshmerga get full marks for trying. The word itself means "those who face death." These patriots or terrorists, depending on your perspective, have been attempting and failing to create a Kurdistan since the 1920s, Saddam Hussein's relationship with the Kurds was complicated, but for the most part, he slaughtered or extorted them. Some of my friend's earliest memories are of fleeing in the dead of night from his town into the countryside to avoid government bombardment. Hussein had a brutal Machiavellian military conscription plan for Kurdish teenagers. Avoiding conscription was a priority because life expectancy was low for a Kurd pressed into Iraqi military service.

At age 16, Ishmael was on a bus headed to school. Government police stopped the vehicle and extracted several Kurdish teenagers, including my friend. He never made it to school, and his parents were never contacted. After two months of military training, he was allowed to call his parents and let them know what had happened to him. At 17, he became a tank gunner in the Iraqi military. He was told that his family would be shot, if he deserted.

The year was 1990. Kuwait was annexed by Iraq, and the world objected. There would be war. My friend's unit mobilized. Since they were under a complete information blackout, they had no idea where they were going or who they might be facing. After days of travel, some began to suspect that they had crossed over into Kuwait.

An undeniable sense of foreboding crept into Ishmael's belly as he and his platoon dug in near what they now suspected to be the Saudi border. Their line of tanks would be the first line of defense if a coalition counterattack came. A few hours before the start of what would become known as the First Gulf War, my friend and a fellow soldier crawled forward a couple of hundred meters in front of their line of tanks. Sweat from nerves and exertion soaked their skin as they scooped tiny foxholes for themselves out of the sand. They were the advance guard. They would be the first to take on fire should it happen. They were supposed to sleep in shifts that night, but neither slept.

The attack came shortly before the sun broke over the desert horizon. It came with lightning quickness and devastating efficiency. Suddenly, the terrifying scream of low-flying aircraft shattered the quiet darkness. My friend could feel the whoosh of their wind currents as they rushed by, followed by the deafening concussion of their ordinance. The entire front line of tanks was obliterated. This was no fair fight. This was a massacre. In mere moments all that remained was burning wreckage and broken bodies scattered everywhere. Miraculously, Ishmael survived the hellish inferno. If he hadn't been 200 meters in front of everyone else, he would not have been so fortunate. His friend survived as well, but not unscathed; a piece of shrapnel had struck him in the head. Blood soaked into the soft sand as my friend quickly bandaged the wound. Ishmael then crammed the wounded soldier's helmet back down onto his head and strapped it on as tightly as he could. Blood was already starting to ooze through the bandaging and down the man's forehead. "Don't take your helmet off for any reason," was the only medical advice my friend could give.

When dawn finally arrived, it became apparent that the front line had been broken. The highest-ranking officer who had managed to survive the slaughter gathered up those remaining. He symbolically removed his military shirt and told everyone the Muslim equivalent of "good luck." Retreat was the only possibility for survival; staying and fighting was certain death. The few survivors that remained began picking their way back to Iraq. They soon learned to stay off the roadways, and hide their guns and uniforms. The coalition forces were taking full advantage of air superiority. All military targets, whether advancing or retreating, were fair game. The retreat into Iraq and up to Kurdish regions in the North was a terrifying, harrowing journey, but somehow my friend made it. Eventually, Ishmael was employed by the U.N. as an interpreter in Turkey. After some time he was offered asylum in Canada thanks to his excellent work in the refugee camps. When Ishmael moved to his new country, he changed his last name to Freeman as a symbolic act. Over the years of difficulty and struggle, there were many times when my friend doggedly hung on to the hope that one day he would make it to the West and be a free man. That's what kept him trudging forward in the darkest of nights.

What if there could be an eternal hope that makes the blessings of Western freedom that my friend now experiences pale in comparison? The Christian story happily says this hope exists, and it carries those who believe through their darkest days. Why not believe it? When I asked my friend that very question, he shook his head and let me know that the damage caused by the religion of his birth has made it impossible for him to become attached to any one particular story, especially if it is fastened to organized religion. I try to speak of greater hope, but he cannot hear the message. Organized religions blind people to the truth, he tells me. It's been 30 years since his father struck him, but he still feels the pain. That's his reality; that's his story.

Interestingly, Ishmael said that if he ever had to pick a faith story around which to shape his life he would choose the Christian one because it has the most hope and love. He sees it for what it is, but he cannot as yet step forward into it. For Ishmael, life is straightforward: there are good people and evil people. They fill the ranks of both the religious and the irreligious. Righteousness for him is to work hard, help the worthy, punish the wicked, be a good neighbour, and — as much as possible — live in peace. Living a good life before whatever God there might be does not involve going to a church or mosque or signing on to some structured system. These things are unnecessary and even unhelpful in living out his vision of what matters. Specifics on God, Jesus, and the afterlife are guesswork. They are topics for engaging conversations over a beer with the hockey game playing in the background, but nothing to get overly serious about.

My friend is a "Freeman," but he is still enslaved by his PTSD, and endures seasons of intense discouragement and darkness. In those moments, solace from God does not come; what does help are good friends who can be with him in those dark moments. Is he missing something in his life that only God can fill? That's not how he sees it. For him, a mortal cage is a tolerable place to live, especially if you reside in the free world and surround yourself with good friends. The only cage to worry about is the one created by oppressive people, cultures, and systems of belief. My friend makes a lot of sense, and with his agnostic, hard-working, good person, help-others perspective, the bars of his mortal cage don't seem so depressing.

Chapter 5

Madness in the Middle East:
If God is dead, he must surely have died trying to fix the Jewish-Arab problem

There was a crisis and I got to be the hero. Two toddlers at the park had slipped through a crack in the fence and were headed for the road. The moms could not slip through the crack or climb the fence, and by the time they could run all the way around to the gate, it would be too late to stop their kids from wandering into the street. I sprang into action, launching myself over the fence and scooping up the wee ones just in time. Whew! The moms were grateful, the toddlers learned a valuable lesson, and everyone clapped. After the high drama at the playground was over, I plopped myself down by my Jewish friend, whom I will call Jacob. He is big, strong, and crusty.

"Dennis, I was watching your heroics" he began. "I have to tell you, if those were Jewish kids, I would have jumped the fence to save them. If they were Christian kids, I might have jumped the fence to save them. But if they were Muslim kids, I would have let them get hit by a car."

I slapped him on the arm and said, "That's terrible! You care more about ethnic loyalty than about doing what's right!" He shrugged his shoulders. I continued my righteous chastening: "As long as you believe that, there will never be peace."

"Who said I want peace?" he replied.

To make his point, for the next several minutes, Jacob described in heart-wrenching detail everything the Jewish people have suffered over the last century at the hands of Muslims and other anti-Semitic peoples. He concluded his sobering lecture with a few choice current atrocities against Jews that had recently happened in the Middle East.

"Dennis, wake up!" he urged me. "Peace is not possible. Those people don't want it. They want the Jews buried at the bottom of the Mediterranean Sea. So we will take what is ours and learn to manage the situation. We are very good at that."

Later that night, he sent me a video of a Taliban soldier executing a woman in the street. She appeared to be coming home from a shopping trip. She knew she was in trouble and began pleading with the man who had accosted her. He didn't listen. She started praying loudly, hands in the air. The man made the woman kneel in the street as onlookers gathered to watch. Methodically, he pulled out his Glock and put it to the back of the woman's head; for a few seconds, he appeared to be lecturing her, as a father might chide a daughter who had spilled some milk. Then he pulled the trigger. The woman slumped down into the street, her head quickly becoming an island in a pool of her own blood.

I was horrified. I shut the video off and shook my head in disbelief. This must be doctored, right? What was her crime anyway? In a text, my Jewish friend told me that she had been executed because her head covering had too many colours in it. "These are the kinds of people my people have to work with," he said. "There is no working with them; they are animals. They are nothing like us, so there can be no peace. Even the 'peaceful' ones still support these insane people. I hate them all," he concluded.

Jacob's story of a Jewish homeland for Jews is all that matters; that's his transcendent cause. The good guys are the ones that help the Jews, and the bad guys are the ones who don't. As far as the Torah is concerned, the guiding principle is that the Jews are God's chosen, so they must be protected and preserved at all costs.

While my wife Mistin and I were cultivating a friendship with Jacob and his family, we also had the unique opportunity to host a young female student from Saudi Arabia, whom I will call AJ. She stayed with us for an entire year. As an ardent Muslim, she wore a niqab (which covered all of her face but her eyes), prayed five times a day, and was zealous to proselytize for Islam. As with most Muslims I know, she was very open to talking about faith and religion. We had many talks that year, during which I discovered in her a profound hatred of the Jews. This was a beautiful, educated, articulate woman who, out of one side of her mouth would expound Islam as a religion of peace, then out of the other side tell me that the Jewish people were a virus that needed to be eradicated. When I questioned her on the inconsistency of a peaceful religion that also wanted to exterminate the Jews, she told me that there was no inconsistency because Islam is only violent in defense of itself. And according to Allah, self-defense is a righteous action.

"So Islam never conquers; it only defends?" I asked.

"That's right, the Jews are the ones who conquer. They are the ones who control everything."

I had just finished reading the book *A Concise History of the Middle East* by Arthur Goldschmidt and Lawrence Davidson. I learned about the mind-boggling conquests of the Muslim empire from the 7th to 13th centuries. From the very beginning, Muhammed conquered Mecca and built expansion into the fabric of his religious system. I took AJ over to our wall-sized world map in our dining room and began to recount the expansion of Islam to her. "Was the conquest of the Levant defensive?" I asked as I pointed to the Middle East. "Or the conquest of North Africa from Egypt to the Atlantic Ocean and then up into Spain? What about eastward expansion from the Arabian Peninsula to Indonesia? Was the centuries-long campaign to conquer Constantinople, the heart of the Christian world, purely defensive as well?"

She folded her arms, raised her eyebrows, and shrugged her shoulders. "Yes, it must have all been defensive!" she said.

I kept pointing at the map, gesturing at the size of Muslim expansion during those centuries. She would not see these as conquests. At this point, I unwisely began sharing with her some of the less noble parts of Muhammad's life. There is nothing like throwing shade on the hero of someone's story to try to win them over to your point of view. I had the foolish thought that she would not show such devotion to Allah's man if she knew a little more dirt about him. The attempt to tarnish Muhammad's image failed miserably. The conversation ended when she threatened jihad on me in my own home if I would not stop denigrating the prophet, *peace be upon him.*

In their book, Goldschmidt and Davidson suggest that if God is dead, it must surely be because he died trying to fix the Jewish-Arab problem. After meeting Jacob and AJ, and seeing how deeply their histories and stories have shaped their views of the other's culture, I agree.

One day, we invited Jacob and his family over to our house to teach us how to cook falafel. We knew it was a risky move. What would happen if Jacob and AJ bumped into each other?

AJ arrived home from school and plopped herself down at the dining room table. At the same moment, Jacob burst through the back door with a big smile wearing his bright blue "Israel 1948 and Forever" T-shirt. They locked eyes and tension filled the air. Mistin and I sprang into action. Standing back-to-back between them, we managed to keep things civil. Even so, AJ was not interested in joining us for dinner; after a few minutes of strained conversation, she retired upstairs and locked herself in her bedroom, re-emerging only after Jacob was gone.

For a year with AJ, and several years with Jacob, we attempted to share the gospel of peace. We tried to model it and speak it when opportunities arose. We wanted them to receive and understand a better story of forgiveness in Christ. However, even if they agreed with me, neither could forgive. They can't believe in a better story because too much blood has already been spilled. They feel the guilty must pay, and so the cycle goes on and on and on. This is their reality; this is their story.

Thinking about the history of humanity, I understand their hesitations. I feel like a loser talking of forgiveness and hope in Jesus from my comfortable perch in a free, prosperous, and peaceful Western country. I am like a kid entering into a grown-up conversation. How could I possibly understand? How could a simple story about Jesus dying and forgiving everybody even remotely make any difference in the Jewish-Arab controversy? It sounds like nonsense in their ears. These are major league problems, and it feels like I can only offer a minor league solution. For Jacob, life is about staying faithful to your people—the Jewish people the Chosen Ones, as he reminds me with great regularity. Righteousness is whenever someone helps a Jew. Unrighteousness is whenever someone doesn't. Truth is a tool, helpful when needed and disregarded when not. Loyalty is all that matters. Getting what you need for your people to survive and thrive is what life is all about. Adequately managing the outsiders is the key to success.

"And what of God?" I ask my friend.

"Well of course he supports the Jews, just like you should."

AJ's and Jacob's beliefs have been shaped by the difficult circumstances of their lives. If there is genuinely a better story, they cannot hear it. The call to Jihad rings too loudly for one, and the rocket attack air raid sirens block any good news for the other. For millennia, Jews and Arabs have done what they had to do to survive. Survival means war and suffering, and even though both are religious, God seems either disinterested or content to let the carnage continue. AJ prays for the destruction of the Jews, and

Jacob for the destruction of the Arabs. With all the prayers of murder and death going up, it is hard to envision a better story coming down. I feel this intractable dilemma deeply, and this is only one example of the never-ending human struggle. It is unrelenting, as are the doubts these questions elicit. Prayers to God make little difference. The true story is the struggle to survive. Humans use religion as a means to power, nothing more. Thoughts like these grow louder and louder in my ears until they shove me unceremoniously back into the mortal cage.

Chapter 6

Sex:
Christianity's Achilles' heel

*They were right. I was wrong to call sexual abuse in the
Southern Baptist Convention (SBC) a crisis.
Crisis is too small a word. It is an apocalypse.*
Russell Moore

Christian leaders will tell you that the grand story of God is wonderful, and I agree. Belief in a creator gives a sense of purpose and identity. Faith in a saviour enables humanity to forgive, worship, and love. Trust in the indwelling spirit of God gives us a profound power source outside of ourselves that fortifies us to change for the better without the unhelpful baggage of pride. The better story's hope-filled vision of a restoration of all things allows us to keep going amid adverse circumstances.

But where does sex fit in with the story? For the most part, the answer for nearly 2,000 years of Christian history has been that it doesn't. Christianity has an abysmal anti-sex track record. When combined with the obscene levels of hypocrisy that have come to light in recent days, it is no surprise that people are heading for the exits of their faith in unprecedented numbers. The Church's catastrophic failure in such a core area of human existence tends to push me back into the cage I've been trying to escape. Humans seem to be beasts at the core. Even if we dress ourselves up in religion, most of us do not seem to be able to reign in our natural tendencies. For the religious, this results in abuse, cover-ups, and eventual scandal. At times it seems best to embrace some version of sexual freedom, where our natural tendencies can live in the open, instead of pretending to be something we are not.

A history of guilt, shame, and radical restraint

Christianity has had a notoriously difficult time figuring out how the desire for Jesus and the desire for sex might work together. The early church fathers simply did not see sex as a reason for praise offered to the creator of pleasure. Origen thought his sexuality would interfere with his spirituality, so he castrated himself. His story of mutilation masquerading as holiness comes to us from fourth century Eusebius, one of the earliest Christian historians:

> At this time, while Origen was conducting catechetical instruction at Alexandria, a deed was done by him which evidenced an immature and youthful mind, but at the same time gave the highest proof of faith and continence. For he took the words, 'There are eunuchs who have made themselves eunuchs

for the kingdom of heaven's sake," Matthew 19:12, in too literal and extreme a sense. And in order to fulfill the Saviour's word, and at the same time to take away from the unbelievers all opportunity for scandal—for, although young, he met for the study of divine things with women as well as men—he carried out in action the word of the Saviour. He thought that this would not be known by many of his acquaintances. But it was impossible for him, though desiring to do so, to keep such an action secret. When Demetrius, who presided over that parish, at last learned of this, he admired greatly the daring nature of the act, and as he perceived his zeal and the genuineness of his faith, he immediately exhorted him to courage, and urged him the more to continue his work of catechetical instruction....the bishops of Cesarea and Jerusalem, who were especially notable and distinguished among the bishops of Palestine, considered Origen worthy in the highest degree of the honour and ordained him a presbyter. Thereupon his fame increased greatly, and his name became renowned everywhere, and he obtained no small reputation for virtue and wisdom.[1]

Eusebius comments that Origen was "immature" and "extreme," but he doesn't condemn his actions. The maiming of Origen's genitalia was proof of the integrity of his faith. This violent action against his sexual anatomy launched his career as a minister. Who could criticize him? After all, it was Jesus who said, in Matthew 5:29, "So if your eye—even your good eye—causes you to lust, gouge it out and throw it away. It is better for you to lose one part of your body than for your whole body to be thrown into hell." For Origen, the offending member was not his eye, but the point was clear: to serve Jesus in the purest way possible, his genitalia had to go!

Augustine, in the *Confessions*, bemoans the fact that one day at the public baths, his father noticed the "signs of active virility coming to life in me."[2] His dad, a non-Christian, joked about the possibility of grandchildren one day from his embarrassed 16-year-old son. Augustine's mother, a Christian, did not see the humour in the innocent erection. She told her son with great fear and seriousness that he was never to "commit fornication and above all not to seduce any man's wife." Augustine did not take his mom's advice, and throughout his youth, he was "tossed and spilled, floundering in the broiling sea of [his] fornication."[3] Years later, as he recounts those tumultuous days of sexual excess, he strings together several scriptures to help his readers see what would have been the better way:

> That a man does well to abstain from all commerce with women (1 Corinthians 7:1) and that he who is unmarried is concerned with God's claim, asking how he is to please God; whereas the married man is concerned with the world's claim, asking how he is to please his wife (1 Corinthians 7:32-33). These were the words to which I should have listened with more care, and if I had made myself a eunuch for love of the kingdom of heaven (Matthew 19:12) I should have awaited your embrace with all the greater joy.[4]

The only difference between Origen's perspective and Augustine's was that Origen had the chutzpah to go all the way.

In *Redeeming Sex*, Deborah Hirsh recounts even more examples of godly men expressing remarkable animosity towards sexual activity. Ambrose, who converted Augustine, encouraged married priests to "stop having sex with [their] wives", so they could focus on loving God. The early church historian Jerome was utterly convinced that Mary, the mother of Jesus, could not have had a sex life, as it would sully her perfect reputation. Augustine built an entire theology against the use of private parts by suggesting that original sin was passed on by having sex. Second-century Saint Clement of Alexandria restricted his church members to unenjoyed procreative sex only during the nighttime hours. The basic assumption of the early church was the more sex, the more sin. Therefore, sex should be avoided as much as possible if one hopes to become more spiritual.[5]

Over time, even the verses in the Bible that promote sexual activity got a radical reinterpretation to better fit an increasingly anti-sex view. For example, Augustine shows astonishing interpretive creativity with God's command in Genesis, "Be fruitful and multiply":

> I take the reproduction of humankind to refer to the thoughts which our minds conceive because reason is fertile and productive. I am convinced that this is what was meant, O Lord, when you commanded man and the creatures of the sea to increase and multiply.[6]

As Christianity expanded, so did its ignorance, fear, and guilt surrounding sex. Eventually, the Church declared even marital sex for pleasure a "venial" sin. In other words, it wouldn't send you to hell if you did it, but it certainly wouldn't point you in the direction of heaven. Sex, through the era of Christendom, was reduced to the status of "necessary evil." Of course, there were voices against this "less is more" idea of sex: Martin Luther, for one,[7] and prominent Puritan Richard Baxter for another. Baxter advised, "Take delight in your wife and keep up your sexual love in a constant heat and vigour."[8] But these voices were largely overshadowed.

Throughout the Middle Ages, church leaders were doing everything they could to forbid sex. According to Hirsch, they tried to implement rules based on the church calendar to help edge out the possibility of copulation. No sex for forty days before Christmas. No sex for forty days before and eight days after Easter. No sex for eight days after Pentecost. No sex on the eves of feast days. No sex on Sundays in honour of the resurrection. No sex on Wednesdays to call to mind the beginning of Lent. No sex on Fridays in memory of the crucifixion. No sex during pregnancy and no sex for thirty days after birth (forty if the child is female). No sex during menstruation and no sex five days before communion!

This adds up to 252 "no sex allowed" days, not counting feast days. Throw in 30 more feast days, and all you have left is 83 days in the year to have sex...provided that the woman did not happen to be menstruating or pregnant or in the post-natal period and that the interlude was intended for procreation only.[9] With this system, you could strike out for years at a time! No wonder so many wars erupted throughout the Middle Ages—everyone was miserable!

Christianity's deep mistrust of all things sexual continued into the modern era and is alive and well in many contemporary Christian circles. Take this alarming example from Simon Winchester's book *The Madman and the Professor:*

William Chester Miner was certifiably insane, but he was also brilliant. He was raised in the home of a Congregational minister in the mid-1800s on the island of Ceylon, known today as Sri Lanka. He was sent back to the United States to pursue further education as a young teenager. From early on, Miner exhibited a significant sexual appetite. His Christian roots made it impossible for him to discuss his sexual struggles openly or satiate them in any appropriate way, so he remained shackled by fear, guilt, and shame. Finally, at Yale, he dispensed with his faith to fully indulge his sexual addictions without the accompanying fear or guilt. He pronounced himself an atheist and beat a steady path into whatever red-light districts happened to be closest to him. His studies led him to become a surgeon, and as circumstances would have it, he volunteered to serve as a captain in the American Civil War. Sadly, his sensitive mind could not adequately handle the trauma of battle. In particular, Miner was given the grizzly task of branding deserters in the face with a hot iron. This brutality, combined with the unhealthy effects of his sexual addictions, caused him to lose his mind. He became a paranoid lunatic. In 1872 Miner's mental instability led him to shoot and kill George Merritt, a poor factory worker and father of seven. The murder took place in England and caused an international scandal that filled the papers on both sides of the Atlantic. Miner was declared criminally insane and interned at Broadmoor Lunatic Asylum in England.

As Miner passed 60 years of age, he found himself open to the idea of God again, through the influence of his Christian friend Dr. James Murray. Murray intended Miner to experience solace and comfort through reawakened faith. Sadly, that's not what happened. The age-old struggle between Christianity and sex filled Miner's tormented mind. He solved the issue as only an insane man could.

"He suddenly stopped thinking of his insanity as a treatable sadness and instead took to thinking of it as an intolerable affliction, a state of sin that needed constant purging and punishment. He began to regard himself not as a sorry creature, but as someone inexpressively vile, endowed with dreadful habits and leanings. He was, in any case, a compulsive and obsessive masturbater and

God would be certain to punish him dreadfully. Sexual pleasure and fantasy had given him as much pleasure as anything else in the world, but when he became Christianized, he saw that he must sever himself from the lascivious life that he had been leading and decided that the amputation of his penis would solve the problem. When the deed was done, he cast his offending member into the fireplace and called for the warden to take him to the infirmary."[10]

Should Miner be faulted for his desire to escape the punishing hand of God via such extreme measures? Is this a virtuous story of overcoming temptation through radical obedience? No, it's a terrible story, and herein lies the problem. The bloody end to this disturbing tale has its roots deep in Christianity.

In my own life, I remember the crushing guilt and shame that I experienced as I came into my sexual awareness. I can still remember the feeling of impending doom that I felt the first time I woke up a bit prematurely from a night dream and finished the job. I knew that something sexual had happened and that it must be a terrible sin, even though it was enjoyable. "One strike," I thought to myself. Perhaps God might give me three strikes before he unleashed his terrible fury upon me. Sermons from the pulpit and warnings from youth group only enhanced my fear of God's righteous wrath upon me. Anything sexual happening to me was very bad indeed, unless, of course, I was married. But I was only 13.

I experienced another strike not long after, when I saw down the shirt of the braless cashier clerk at a local convenience store. I was utterly undone by the sight of this forbidden pleasure as she leaned over the counter to receive my money. Needless to say, it wasn't long before all my strikes were used up and then some! As a Christian teenager, I lived in perpetual guilt, fear, shame, and ignorance surrounding my sexuality. I simply did not know how to understand it, and there was no one I could talk to. In Christian history, I can easily see the path that led me to be a confused, shame-filled, guilt-ridden Christian teen who had no idea what to do with his sexuality.

Hypocrisy of epic proportions

This unfortunate history now joins hands with an unprecedented level of hypocrisy. Christians are notoriously ineffective at keeping their own guidelines. In December 2018, Christianity Today ran an article commenting on a major investigative report produced by the Fort Worth Star-Telegram. The report uncovered 412 allegations of sexual abuse across nearly 200 churches in the independent fundamentalist movement. This group is the most vocal and bombastic in its objections to even minor advances in sexual freedom. Yet, upon acquiring positions of power and influence, many of its leaders can't help themselves from dipping into the sweet honey of infidelity, immorality, adultery, homosexuality, and everything else they so rigorously preach against. Many of the incidents were covered up, and in cases of abuse, perpetrators were never brought to justice, further devaluing the Jesus story in the eyes of the broader culture.

Catholics continue to face one damning revelation after another. Just type "Catholic sex abuse scandal" into a web browser and you will have innumerable examples of Christian hypocrisy in this area. Watch the 2015 movie *Spotlight*, which follows the true story of a team of investigative journalists who uncover decades of sexual abuse in the Catholic Church. Celibacy for ministry leaders in this stream of faith is built upon the faulty premise that having a sex life is a deterrent to godliness. The staggering body count of sexually abused within the Catholic faith tells us all we need to know about the wisdom of this line of thinking.

The list of prominent evangelicals who have said one thing about sex and done the opposite continues to grow, especially in the wake of the #metoo movement. The list is depressingly impressive: Ravi Zacharius, Paige Patterson, Ted Haggard, Bill Hybels, Bruxy Cavey, and pretty much all of the Southern Baptist Convention![11] Evangelicals of all kinds are regularly exposed for actions that go against any "better story" that promotes some measure of sexual restraint.

Everyday Christians do not seem to be faring any better. Porn addiction among Christian men rings in at 70% or higher. These stats are easily accessed through a half dozen or so Christian websites that monitor this kind of stuff. Christian pastors are a little better, trailing not far behind at 50%. The utopian vision of sexual freedom has saturated society to such a degree that only the most vigilant Christians among us don't bow the knee to its tantalizing appeal. Promiscuity and infidelity happen within church communities with unrelenting regularity. One dismal poll listed "no statistical difference" in the lifestyle activities of believers versus non-believers when looking at a list of ten traditionally non-Christian vices.[12]

A 2007 Barna Group study revealed the top three reasons people reject Christianity: Christianity is too anti-homosexual, judgmental, and hypocritical.[13]

When the adherents of a particular worldview cannot follow its guidelines with any degree of consistency, eventually it will be swept aside. Many Christians, myself included, have found themselves hand-cuffed by confusing, retrograde views on sex that inevitably result in hypocritical behaviour. For untold numbers, it is just too much. Being a Christian has become embarrassing. The feeling is captured perfectly by those old Southwest Airlines commercials. Someone does something stupid, creating a chagrining mess. "Wanna get away?" the narrator deadpanes as the camera surveys the unfortunate scene. For increasing numbers of Christians, the answer is an unequivocal yes.

In my 23 years of professional ministry, the confusion, criticism, and chaos around this thorny issue has caused more people to keep the Christian faith at arm's length—or leave it altogether—than anything else by far.

End Notes:

[1] See http://people.ucalgary.ca/~vandersp/Courses/texts/eusebius/eusehe6.html#VI - Digital copy of Eusebius Book 6, Chapter 8

[2] Augustine, *Confessions* - Kindle, (London England: Penguin Books, 1961), 45.

[3] Ibid., 43.

[4] Ibid., 44.

[5] Debra Hirsch, *Redeeming Sex*, (Downers Grove, IL: InterVarsity Press, 2015). The examples in this paragraph are scattered throughout chapter two of Debra Hirsch's book.

[6] Augustine, *Confessions*, 336.

[7] See https://www.patheos.com/blogs/geneveith/2015/06/luther-on-sex/ In a letter to his friend Nicolas Gerbal, Luther said, "We are permitted to laugh and have fun with and embrace our wives, whether they are naked or clothed." The idea of priestly celibacy to him was a terrible idea that would only produce "division, sin, shame, and scandal to be increased without end."

[8] Gary Thomas, *Sacred Marriage* (Grand Rapids Mich.: Zondervan, 2015), 204.

[9] Ibid.,202.

[10] Simon Winchester, *The Professor and the Madman* (Newark NJ: Audible, 1999), Chapter 9, starting at the 27th minute.

[11] This comment about the SBC is an exaggeration. What isn't an exaggeration is former SBC leader Russell Moore's characterization of the 2022 report on sex scandals and cover-ups within the Southern Baptist denomination as "apocalyptic."

[12] Mark Clark, The Problem of God (Grand Rapids Mich.: Zondervan, 2017), 185.

[13] Ibid, 181.

Part Two
Escape

As I reached my mid-40s, my internal doubts and misgivings regarding my faith continued to increase. External conversations with my friends—many of whom were living lives far more complicated and raw than I had ever imagined as a young Christian—only strengthened the bars that were fixing themselves around me. An almost total experiential blackout from God didn't help matters either. And finally, that whole sex thing made me think I should just get comfortable in my mortal cage.

But I didn't get comfortable; instead, a bit of a jailbreak happened. It hasn't been a clean break. There are times I still feel stuck in the mortal cage. Doubts and skepticism never completely go away. But despite the years of defeat and silence, a new hope has begun to rise in my soul. In this next section I will trace out ten discoveries I have found along the way that have freed me from the cage and helped me to cautiously embrace a reality beyond its bars.

Chapter 7

Some help from the doubters

Faith is fraught; confession is haunted by an inescapable sense of its contestability. We don't believe instead of doubting; we believe while doubting. We're all Thomas now.
James K.A. Smith

I do believe; help my unbelief!
Mark 9:24

Not everybody struggles with terrible, faith-upending doubts. Augustine, the great-granddaddy of Western Christianity, declares that his doubts fled away after his conversion. Unquestionably, the preaching of his mentor, the educated and highly regarded Ambrose, helped give Christianity the intellectual street cred

Augustine needed to cross over into belief. But this is not the whole story. Divine interventions also underpinned Augustine's conversion: God healed him of a toothache. The power of a song in a church service "entered his ears and filled his heart." He witnessed a season of persecution end when the bodies of two ancient martyrs were discovered and paraded through the streets. The healing powers of these holy corpses cast out demons, healed a blind man, and stopped the persecution in its tracks. Augustine could not deny these miraculous experiences. He became convinced that the love of God was real and open to him, so he entered into the Christian faith and never looked back.[14]

I am happy for Augustine. I have often wished I had his certainty, his lived experience, and the confidence in God's love that shines through his *Confessions*. But I don't. It turns out I am more of a Dostoevsky man myself.

In a moment of candour, Russian philosophical novelist Fyodor Dostoevsky penned these words in a letter to a good friend:

> I want to say to you, about myself, that I am a child of this age, a child of unfaith and skepticism, and probably (indeed I know it) shall remain so to the end of my life. How dreadfully has it tormented me (and torments me even now) this longing for faith.[15]

It is no surprise that, in his classic novel *The Brothers Karamazov*, Dostoevsky creates a tortured soul in his own image named Ivan.

Ivan can never make peace with his doubts. Family friend

Rakitin says of him, "He has a stormy spirit. His mind is in bondage. He is haunted by a great, unsolved doubt. He is one of those who doesn't want millions but an answer to their questions."[16]

Ivan's unsolved questions turn into festering doubts, which in turn destroy his ability to believe in a good God, absolute truth, or even love. "All is lawful," he laments, summarizing his belief that the world is a dark place without meaning, morality, or God. In the end, the darkness of Ivan's doubts takes active root in his servant and provides the underling with the justification to murder Ivan's father and frame Ivan's brother for the crime. When the shocked Ivan queries his servant about his heinous deeds the answer comes crashing back on him: "All is lawful."

Ivan, caught in the clutches of doubt, hopelessness, and despair, cannot seem to escape this soul-crushing trap. He knows that faith in a loving God will provide deliverance from his bleak outlook. He even has in his life an example of the liberating power of trust in God—his saintly brother, Alyosha. But Ivan cannot bring himself to step into the realm of belief. Faith, for Ivan, is too simple, too easy. He has seen too much of the way things are. He has, as my non-Christian friend quipped one day on a long walk together, "seen how the sausage is made" when it comes to religion. Ivan remains entombed in his tortured reality.

I identify with Ivan. With frustrating regularity, I find myself tortured by those "great unsolved" doubts about my faith. Is my faith proof that I am a weak-minded person playing a silly game to cope with life? I wonder with increasing perplexity if I am missing something. Is the truth about life and religion revealed in Phillip Larkin's clever verse?

No trick dispels. Religion used to try, That vast moth-eaten musical brocade Created to pretend we never die.[17]

Have the infamous Thénardiers grasped the truth about our existence as they stumble around picking the pockets of the dead in the Broadway musical *Les Misérables*? They are convinced that the world is a dog-eat-dog place. Humans have to kill for the bones in the streets just like dogs do, and nobody will do anything about it, least of all God, because he is as dead as the people the dogs help themselves to. As the song crescendos, this ragtag bunch of opportunistic thieves declares that when they lift their eyes to the heavens, only the moon shines down.

Ironically, Dostoevsky and other chronic doubters like him have helped revive my faith because they have permitted me to struggle. Growing up in a stringent version of Christianity, I was taught early on that any sort of doubt was tantamount to unbelief. It needed to be stamped out immediately with the loud singing of hymnic anthems, the vigorous signing of doctrinal statements, the aggressive defense of the faith through evidentialist apologetics, and the often-angry proof-texting of Scripture. I did all of these things, none of which helped long-term. In the end, learning to allow myself the freedom to doubt amidst belief has been the single most significant discovery that has allowed my faith to remain.

Samuel Taylor Coleridge, the famed 19th-century British poet, lifelong doubter, and superstar in the fraternity of uneasy believers, has been helpful. His immortal poem, "The Rime of the Ancient Mariner," is an epic retelling of the poet's troubled, doubt-filled life.

The mariner's journey out to sea and back again reflects

Coleridge's own loss and recovery of faith among the thunderclouds of doubt and misgiving.

Coleridge lost his father at age 13. The tragedy compounded when he was yanked away from the comforts of nature and family, and stuffed into an ultra-strict boarding school in the cloistered brick and dust of London. When he developed rheumatic fever as a teenager, London's medical minds prescribed what was thought to be a tremendous new cure-all from the Far East: opium. Amidst the rubble of lifelong drug addiction that destroyed most of his relationships, the "enlightened" minds of his day urged Coleridge to abandon his faith, the only thing helping him see beyond the dark malaise of his existence. Coleridge acknowledged that "a sort of calm hopelessness defused itself over [his] heart" for long stretches of his life.

But he did not falter completely. He longed to see the world around him not as a blank wall, but as a door or a window to the divine. Coleridge's gift to uneasy believers like me was the freedom he gave himself to doubt openly. As he said later in life, "My wandering through the wilderness of doubt has enabled me to skirt without crossing the sandy deserts of utter unbelief."[18]

I am like Dostoevsky, Coleridge, Smith, and the poor guy from Mark 9 who both believed in Jesus and did not at the same time. Thanks to these doubters, I am less concerned about having these opposites dwell together within me. I now see that simultaneous doubt and belief are more of a gift than a curse. I understand the tension it produces as a spiritual workout that makes me both stronger and more honest. I wrestle in the open now; I have good and not so good moments of faith—and that is okay. This freedom to doubt prevents me from becoming a strutting over-confident

Christian, someone I don't want to be. Embracing doubt as my friend has done the most important thing of all. As Coleridge says, it has kept me out of the sandy deserts of utter unbelief. It has allowed me to escape the mortal cage.

End Notes:

[14] Augustine, *Confessions*, 181-200.

[15] Letter To Mme. N. D. Fonvisin (1854), as published in Letters of Fyodor Michailovitch Dostoevsky to his Family and Friends (1914), translated by Ethel Golburn Mayne, Letter XXI, 71.

[16] Fyodor Dostoevsky, Translated by Constance Garnett, *The Brothers Karamazov* (Mineola, New York: Dover Books, 2005), 189.

[17] Philip Larkin, Aubade 3rd Stanza. See https://www.poetryfoundation.org/poems/48422/aubade-56d229a6e2f07

[18] Malcolm Guite, *A Voyage with Samuel Taylor Coleridge, Mariner* (London, England: Hodder & Stoughton, 2017), 309.

Chapter 8

Faith is what drives us all

> *One can believe that faith is mere credulous assent to unfounded premises, while reason consists in a pure obedience to empirical fact, only if one is largely ignorant of both.*
> David Bentley Hart

"Based on a true story." When I see those words at the beginning of a movie or a book, I'm totally in. Why? It's not made up; it happened. It's true! There are facts involved. For me, the story is worth more if it's factually accurate. NBC news anchor Brian Williams lost his job because he wasn't careful about the truth. He told viewers the helicopter he was flying in was hit by rocket fire—but it turns out it wasn't. He fabricated the scary incident to sensationalize the story and boost his reputation as a frontline reporter. The fib cost him his Nightly News anchor position, his reputation, and his multi-million-dollar salary! Even in our post-modern world, where truth has become relative and malleable, we humans took serious offense when Williams fudged his story. Somehow truth still matters.

But herein lies a dirty trick. We simply cannot know the truth with clinical certainty on the matters of most importance.

How did I get here? Who am I? Is there a purpose? Why should I care? Is death the end? Why is there guilt? Does absolute truth exist? What is love? Is there a God? Does evil exist? These are the questions that drive our core values, motivate our passions, and help us make decisions to act well in the world—and yet we can't know the answers with certainty. We don't know the truth, so we must supplement knowing with faith.

In our world, you can know the truth about how a toaster works or what exactly goes into your hot dog (though you might not want to know). But if you want concrete answers on the huge stuff, the stuff that shapes the direction of your life, you can't get it. All the big questions cannot be answered with a straight-up, "This is true, but this is false." None of us, not atheist-evangelist Richard Dawkins, not the Pope, not you, not me, can find the answers to these questions with air-tight certainty.

One day, a woman walked by me as I sat on a bench at a local city park. I could see that her bare arm had provided a canvas for art and the opportunity had not been lost. I noticed a massive tattoo of the Buddha covering the bulk of her upper arm as she ambled by. I thought to myself, "What does this woman actually know of the Buddha?" It is unlikely that she knows much of anything about him. Perhaps she heard a soundbite about him; maybe she even watched a Netflix original or listened to a podcast. Somehow, over the course of her meagre twenty-some years of existence, she had come to embrace Buddhism enough for its influence to leave a permanent mark.

That got me thinking: what do I know about Jesus? Or better yet: what did I know of him when I started following him as a teenager? Certainly not more than the branded Buddha devotee at the park. This is one of the great ironies of being a human. We chart the direction of our life; we pick whom we listen to and follow; we decide what is good and what is not; we do it all without any substantive knowledge. An uninformed, faith-filled start is how life begins for every human being. We fumble our way forward trying to make sense of things, trying to find answers, trying to discover the truth, trying to chart the course of our life. But we take to the skies on nothing other than the wings of faith.

Yann Martel, in his famous book *Life of Pi*, summarizes the indispensability of faith in the life of every human: "Atheists are my brothers and sisters of a different faith, and every word they speak speaks of faith. We all go as far as the legs of reason will carry us, and then we jump!"[19]

The domain of faith is the human's natural habitat. The question has never really been if we as humans believe in something; it has only always been what or who we might believe in. As writer and philosopher James K. A. Smith says, "So before we are thinkers, we are believers. Before we can offer our rational explanations of the world, we have already assumed whole constellations of belief."[20]

Theologian David Bentley Hart puts it this way:

All reasoning presumes premises or intuitions or ultimate convictions that cannot be proved by any foundations or facts more basic than themselves, and hence there are irreducible convictions present wherever one attempts to apply logic to experience. One always operates within boundaries established by one's (unprovable) first principles and asks only the questions that those principles permit.[21]

These "first principles" that Hart speaks of are in no way strictly rational, purely factual, or consistently scientific. Always and for everyone, explanations of the big questions of life proceed from faith. Or, in Martel's words, "The world isn't just the way it is; it's how we understand it."[22]

American Biblical scholar Peter Enns chimes in: "Few if any come to faith in God by the sheer force of an argument. We come to faith for all sorts of reasons that aren't really reasons at all in the conventional sense. Our 'reasons' are intuitive more than rational, emotional more than logical and mysterious more than known."[23] The lens through which we see our world is built from the glass of faith.

What a liberating realization it is to see that every human on the planet is an ardent believer. For years I felt a bit embarrassed about my faith. I had to pump myself up to speak out because a "faith reveal" seemed somehow unnatural or inappropriate. Showing off my faith in such a fact-based, scientific, rational world is like leaving the washroom with a toilet paper tail; it's just not cool. But faith resides in everyone. The relationship between faith, reason, and truth is complicated, but unquestionably, everyone's explanations for "the way things are" flow first from faith-based presuppositions. David Bentley Hart is delightfully correct when he says, "One can believe that faith is mere credulous assent to unfounded premises, while reason consists in a pure obedience to empirical fact, only if one is largely ignorant of both."[24] Even if I wanted to, I could never escape the life of faith—no one can. The question has never been *if* I have faith; it has only ever been *which* faith I have. This has become a great comfort and a pivotal key to unlocking the door to my mortal cage.

End Notes:

[19] Yann Martel, *Life of Pi*, (Toronto, Canada: Random House, 2001), 55.

[20] James K.A. Smith, *Desiring the Kingdom* (Grand Rapids Mich.: Baker Academic, 2009), 43.

[21] David Bentley Hart, *Atheist Delusions* (New Haven, Connecticut: Yale University Press), 101.

[22] Martel, *Life of Pi*, 428.

[23] Peter Enns, *The Sin of Certainty*, (Newark, NJ: Audible), Chapter 2 at 40 min 50 seconds.

[24] Hart, *Atheist Delusions*, 101.

Chapter 9

To be human is to have a story

We are "narrative animals": we define who we are, and what we ought to do, on the basis of what story we see ourselves in.
Charles Taylor

If we are all creatures of faith, what then is the repository into which human faith flows? It is story. To be human is to have a story. Our secular age is not an age of disbelief; it's an age of believing otherwise,[25] says Canadian philosopher Charles Taylor. For Taylor, those who convert to unbelief "because of science" are less convinced by data and more moved by the story science tells and the self-image that comes with it (for example, that rationality equals maturity).[26] Life is not just what is; it is about how we see things. Perspective is our frame of reference, our point of view, our angle. It is the most important faculty we possess because it shapes and governs how we live our lives. Through trace amounts of evidence and bucketloads of faith, we latch on to the overarching stories that shape us.

One day, as I was riding around Vancouver's seawall with my friend, the topic of religion and faith came up. I hit all the main points of the faith story I believed in as we zipped around Stanley Park on our two-wheeled steeds. Creation, sin, Jesus, redemption, love, forgiveness, grace, hope. I gave him the straight goods on the grand story I am attempting to shape my life around. As we finished our ride, I turned to him and asked him what story he believed.

His answer was short and brutal.

"We happened here by chance. Humans destroy each other; that's not wrong, it's just inconvenient. It's why we invented religion — to keep us alive. However, the truth is we are just beasts stuck in a meaningless existence with no right or wrong, stumbling along towards death."

"That's your story?" I asked.

"Yup."

"That's a terrible story."

"Yeah, but it's true."

"Maybe, but maybe not."

By that point in the conversation, I thought about the possibility of convincing my friend about the "facts" of a historical Jesus or the philosophical arguments that exist for God. Instead, what came out was something like this:

"I'm not trying to convince you that the Christian story is necessarily a true story. It might be, just like your story of a meaningless existence and necessary religion might be. The question I want you to ask yourself is, which is the better one? The one with God or the one without God? Believe the better story!" I ended my impromptu speech with, "By the way, mine is way better than yours!"

He laughed and agreed.

At the centre of every person is a story, not a factoid, a proof, or an argument. It's not always apparent which story might be true. Some stories welcome transcendence. Some don't. Regardless, a story is all any of us has.

End Notes:

[25] Smith, *How (Not) to Be Secular: Reading Charles Taylor*, 47.

[26] Ibid., 77.

Chapter 10

Some stories are better than others. One in particular rises above all the rest

Religion might just be true simply because it is beautiful. The Christian religion didn't last so long merely because everyone believed it. It lasted because it makes for a helluva novel — which is pretty close to Tolkien's claim that the gospel is true because it is the most fantastic fantasy, the greatest fairy story ever told.
James K. A. Smith

French philosopher Voltaire, contemplating the senseless death and destruction caused by the great Lisbon earthquake of 1755, struggled to lift the story of humanity above anything but mortal cage meaninglessness. As only he could, he put the grand story of his belief into poetic verse.

What is the verdict of the vastest mind?

Silence: the book of fate is closed to us.
Man is a stranger to his own research;
He knows not whence he comes, nor whither goes.
Tormented atoms in a bed of mud,
Devoured by death, a mockery of fate.[27]

Undoubtedly, our life experiences shape the stories we believe. I sympathize with his conclusions and all the conclusions of my friends in the earlier part of this book. But is Voltaire's belief a good story? A story that, in the long run, helps us to be better humans? A story that breathes hope, gives meaning and leads to flourishing?

There are other stories. For example, Nietzsche disagreed with Voltaire. Meaninglessness was not the ultimate narrative for life. Instead, it was power. In his book *The Anti-Christ*, published in 1888, he combined power with the freshly – minted laws of evolution to come up with this life-shaping gem:

> Pity thwarts the whole law of evolution, which is the law of natural selections. It preserves whatever is ripe for destruction; it fights on the side of those disinherited and condemned by life; by maintaining life in so many of the botched of all kinds, it gives life itself a gloomy and dubious aspect…What is more harmful than any vice? Practical sympathy for the botched and the weak—Christianity.[28]

Hitler took Nietzsche's story and nationalized it. The Holocaust was the result. I don't like these stories! Do you? Not all stories are good. More than anything, I love a good story, but is there one overarching story that seems to rise above the rest?

She was Saudi. We did not know her very well, but well enough to know she was in trouble. The neighbourhood drunk had cornered her just on the other side of our fence. He was, for the most part, harmless and probably just wanted to talk, but for our friend, it was clear that he was violating her personal space, and she didn't know what to do. Mistin sprang into action. Out the front door, she ran, calling the girl's name loudly; both she and the drunk tuned to face my wife.

"Amal, there you are! So nice to have you finally arrive. Come in, come in, supper is almost ready."

Amal's look of complete bewilderment slowly shifted to understanding. She realized that a rescue attempt was afoot. Grabbing Mistin's arm with a smile, she accompanied her inside. And so it began, an ever-deepening relationship with this wonderful girl.

Sadly, most Saudis living in Canada are transient. They arrive on study visas paid for by their king, and they must return home once they complete their studies. A couple years after Amal's dramatic rescue by Mistin, her departure date arrived Amal and three of her Saudi friends were leaving to return to their homeland. It was supposed to be an exciting time, but it wasn't. They were going back to full head coverings. Back to close-minded men who would refuse to let them be free to walk where they want and talk to follow their dreams. They were returning to their families, which was of some comfort, but they would sorely miss the freedom they were leaving in Canada.

We decided to throw a going-away party for them. We laughed and joked and ate like kings and queens. We took pictures. Interestingly, the girls did not want photos with my wife or my kids.

They wanted pictures only with me, a man, something forbidden in Saudi Arabia. This was one final act of defiance before heading back into the shadows reserved for the women of that culture.

The women spoke of their religion as good but their culture as bad; however they also quickly pointed out the problems with Canadian culture, bitterly recounting how they had lost a generation of good Saudi men when it had become acceptable to study abroad a couple of decades before. This first wave was lost to the corruptions of the Christian West, they told me.

Since Saudi Arabia is an unashamedly Muslim nation, these girls naturally assumed that Canada must be a Christian nation. Therefore, they blamed on Christianity the moral corruption that had swept away so many of Saudi's finest. I quickly explained that Canada has two worldview stories competing for the allegiance of the masses: Christianity and humanism. They clicked their tongues and shook their heads in disapproval as I explained that humanism rejects the idea of God and any rules that have traditionally come from him. Instead, humanism allows for great freedom to experiment with morality since nothing is necessarily right or wrong in this worldview. Sadly, many people—Christians, Muslims, or anyone attempting a vigorous morality—can be easily swept away into the strong current of moral freedom and experimentation. The lost generation of men had not been swept into Christianity, but into humanism. At this point, one of the girls boldly declared, "Of the two, I choose Christianity."

"Me too," I said.

One of the girls then reflected, "Well, Christianity and Islam are basically the same."

They all agreed that Christianity was very good; it was just that it had been corrupted by men who came along after Jesus and blurred his message. Mohammed, I was told, was sent as the prophet destined to correct these errors, and bring the misguided monotheists (Jews and Christians) back to the truth. The girls communicated clearly to me that Islam was, in their estimation, simply a more perfect version of Christianity—a better story. As we discussed the two great faith stories, the similarities became obvious. Both believe that God created all things; that humanity fell into sin; that God has certain standards of morality; and that one day, God would return to set things back in order and judge everyone. As we talked, the girls were smiling broadly. "See," one of them said, "we are the same."

But then it was time to talk about Jesus. This notion that Jesus is God in the flesh was blasphemous to the girls. According to their story, God has no face-to-face dealings with humans, nor would he ever become one. Their story puts God far above created things. The job of the human in the story of Islam is to submit to the will of Allah. Obedience to Allah and his prophet Mohammed is all that ultimately matters.

As the conversation started to build, I wasn't sure what to do; the Jesus talk is always a dead end when conversing with Muslims. Both sides have been trained well on this. Inevitably, Muslims will turn the conversation into a complex analysis of the Trinity, or Christians will begin a harsh critique about unpopular Muslim social customs or of the prophet Mohammed himself. When these conversation trails are taken, the discussion inevitably devolves into an argument, and positions become more entrenched.

I did not want our dialogue to go in either of these directions, so I changed the subject. "Wanna hear how Mistin and I fell in love?" I asked. They agreed.

Now, this was a story I could get into! Mistin and I had met on a blind date. That magical evening together created so many sparkles between us that Mistin had gone home and called her mom, saying that if ever she was going to marry a man, it was me. I went home stunned and excited, wondering what had just happened.

Sadly, there was no opportunity for us to cultivate a relationship at that time. In just a few days, I was headed to Bolivia for a few weeks of mission work, and by the time I returned, Mistin would have left for France. She had planned to spend a year there learning French and then moving to North Africa, where she hoped to live. We got together as much as possible in that final week before we went our separate ways, and we loved every moment together.

When I returned from Bolivia, I was miserable without her. The thought of her being overseas indefinitely and never seeing her again was intolerable. Somehow, I needed to track down her phone number. The search was on! I had discovered that Mistin was serving with a mission agency, so I called their home office and in my deepest, most mature-sounding pastoral voice, said, "Hello, my name is Pastor Wilkinson. I understand you have a new missionary on the field in France, and I will need to get her phone number." The plan worked, and soon we were ringing up substantial phone bills. We quickly outgrew our contentment with a long-distance relationship—this kind of love called for drastic action. Within a few weeks of that first phone call, I bought a ring and a plane ticket.

The girls' eyes grew wide at this point. I told them that for the sake of love, I flew to France to sweep my beloved off her feet. While I was there, a small group of us toured together into Spain and Morocco, and finally, on the way back, the magical moment came on a hill overlooking the Mediterranean Sea. I got down on one knee, confessed my undying love, and asked Mistin to marry me. She said yes!

The girls spontaneously erupted with clapping and cheering. They had been hanging onto every word of our dramatic love story. They loved the idea of a man going to great lengths to pursue the woman he loves. Most marriages in Saudi are still arranged, so a romance story of this sort sounded all the more exciting to the girls.

I shifted to another story with one of the Saudi girls at the centre. As everyone listened, I asked one of the girls to imagine that she was trapped in a faraway land with no hope of escape, but a prince decided to cross oceans and climb mountains to stage a daring rescue for the sake of love. I built out the story in a dramatic fashion, and at precisely the right moment, I looked into Amal's eyes and said, "Imagine what it would be like to have this prince face such danger, all so that he could sweep you up into his arms and love you forever."

Caught in the moment's drama, one of the girls stood up in the middle of our dining room, raised her fist in the air, and shouted, "Give me that man!"

We all laughed, then as the laughter died down, I gently said to her, "That man is Jesus."

There was silence. After a moment or two, I continued, "It's the grandest rescue story of all time: God coming for us to scoop us up in his loving arms to take care of us forever. It's the best love story."

There was no objection, harsh criticism, or technical arguments about the Trinity, only quiet contemplation. Jesus' love story had snuck up on them, because that's what it does. The best stories are owned and embraced because they are simply the best stories. They stand alone. They rise above all the rest. Such is the Christian story of a loving, sacrificing, rescuing God.

Islam cannot compete with a cosmic-sized divine love story like this. The story that came from the lips of Muhammed in the seventh century knows very little about love; that story demands submission to a strict and distant God. The girls could see the difference that evening with crystal clarity. Their natural longings for love, which were so obvious as they participated in my story, connected them irrevocably with the divine love I spoke about. That connection will ultimately leave their current story in ruins. Better stories do that.

The time came to go. The tears were flowing freely now. Over these last many months together, we had grown close. They had become part of our family. Even so, goodbye hugs for me were out of the question. They were Saudi Arabian girls, after all! They compromised and allowed the scandalous physical touches of fist bumps as permissible farewell gestures. The last thing we did together before they left was to pray. We prayed that the love story of Jesus Christ would continue to grow in their lives.

A few years passed, and one of these dear ones returned to

Canada. The reunion and renewed friendship were beautiful. Fatima was back pursuing her master's degree and whatever other degree she could convince her country to pay for. Of all the girls, she preferred Canada over Saudi Arabia the most; she would be happy to be a student forever if that is what it would take for her to live in the West. Fatima studied hard, but she was always connecting with our little community during her breaks. She would share meals with us and join in community-building events. On occasion, she would even join us for church. As time passed, Fatima declared that we were her family and that it would no longer be necessary for her to wear the hijab in my presence. She also told me that hugging over fist bumps would be the preferred greeting since we were family members.

As her studies continued, she became more specialized as a research scientist on arthritic hips. One day over dinner, I mentioned that I was having hip replacement surgery. Her eyes got large, and she blurted out, "I want your hips!"

She needed the extracted femoral heads from hip replacement candidates for her research. "All I study are old hips, but you are young; I want your hips!" she said.

Dinner conversations at our house are never dull, but I must say, this was the first time I've ever had anyone desire my hips over spaghetti and meatballs.

My friend pulled some strings, and she got her wish. After my surgery, she kept me supplied with pictures of the excellent scientific work she was doing with my arthritic bone. Thanks to my bone (and many others) and lots of hard work, Fatima's future in Canada looked bright. She would graduate, and then with her degree and her time spent in Canada, she could apply for permanent residency to fulfill her dream of staying in the West.

Dreams, unfortunately, do not always become reality. Just weeks before her graduation, Canada offered some gentle criticism about Saudi Arabia's human rights abuses. The Saudi king was offended. He told Canada to mind its own business. When Canada didn't retract its criticism, the Saudi leader decided he would punish the country by forcing all Saudi students studying in Canada to return home immediately.

Saudi government emails filled Fatima's inbox: "Return, by order of the king. Obey or lose your citizenship." Our friend had put in six years of diligent study and was mere days away from obtaining her master's degree. It didn't matter—the powers over her were demanding that she leave all and come home. Submit or else. I could not help but wonder who was being punished: Canada or Saudi citizens?

I asked if she wanted to try for refugee status. "No," she said. "The government is forcing me to choose between my freedom and family, but I love my family too much to disobey the king. So I will return," she said.

All I could do was shake my head, sharing her disappointment.

"How does this help me love my country?" she asked. "They are alienating the future of our country by making slaves out of us!" I hugged Fatima and prayed for her.

A few days later, I was preparing a sermon about the sacrificial love of Jesus as the best story. I had planned to offer a gentle critique of Islam in the comparison, so I called up my friend. I wanted a Muslim in the room to keep my criticism fair; she agreed to come.

During the sermon, I mentioned that submission to Allah's will is presented as the better story in Islam. My friend agreed. I then suggested that the better story is not one that has us rigidly obeying the rules of a distant deity; instead, it features a God who comes close to us, who, for the sake of love, sacrifices all to rescue humanity.

There is a shortage of love in Islam's story. Ayatollah Khomeini, the man who established the Islamic Republic of Iran in 1979, thought love was irrelevant: "Islam says whatever good there is in this world, it is because of the sword and the shadow of the sword. People can only be made obedient because of the sword; the sword is the key to paradise. Obedience is better than freedom."[29]

Of course, many Muslims would disagree with Khomeini's rhetoric. But as I shared with the audience my friend's sad situation of being recalled to Saudi Arabia, it didn't seem so extreme. As I spoke, she continued to nod her head in agreement and even added some of her thoughts to my talk. When the sermon ended, I called upon everyone to let the love song of Jesus resonate for the unique and wondrous story that it is. I gave all an opportunity to believe it by coming forward to receive communion.

Fatima nudged my mom, whom everyone in the community lovingly called Grandma Carol. "Grandma Carol," she said, "I want to come forward to receive communion." Together hand in hand, they came forward. My wife and I looked into Fatima's eyes as she came to receive the bread and the wine from us.

"This is Jesus' body broken for you; this is Jesus' blood shed for you. Jesus loves you very much," we said.

Fatima smiled in agreement and responded, "God, thank you for the blood of Jesus."

This wonderful person's heart had been captured by the love story of Jesus. Better stories always seem to rise to the top. Sadly, my friend is not free to believe what she wants as we are in the West, so she may face some hard days ahead as the love story of Jesus germinates in her heart.

Love is a better story, and it is the epicentre of the Christian story. Because of love, no matter how many doubts arise in my heart or how much darkness covers our world, I can never fully go back into the mortal cage.

End Notes:

[27] Voltaire, *Poem on the Lisbon Disaster*, 13th stanza. See http://people.whitman.edu/~iversojr/Candide/lisbon.htm

[28] Friedrich Nietzsche, *The Antichrist*, (New York: Alfred A. Knopf Inc., 1918), 47.

[29] Lawrence Wright, *The Looming Tower*, (Newark NJ: Audible, 2017) 2:06:16 Chapter 2.

Chapter 11

Most stories in the West are poached versions of the Christian one

In Europe, the secular had for so long been secularized that it was easy to forget its ultimate origins. To sign up to its premises was unavoidably to become just that bit more Christian.
Tom Holland

"You are poaching Christianity!" My accusation rang through the restaurant, probably a little louder than it should have.

My atheist friend sheepishly grinned and agreed. Daniel loves the Christian story, but belief in the supernatural is impossible for him, so Christian faith is impossible. The true story for him, when pushed, is a sanitized amalgamation of atheist philosophers like Voltaire and Nietzsche, but their conclusions about life are too dark for my happy friend. He rightly has no time for angry and depressed atheist purists, even though he believes on a foundational level what they think. Acting like Jesus is a much better way to live, so the solution to his quandary is piracy: Co-opt all the big ideas, principles, and teachings of Jesus, while at the same time dismiss the overarching story upon which they are built. Can you do that? My friend is.

Most of us just want regular lives that are more happy than sad, so we go with whatever works. Is that a problem? At the moment, it is working for my friend.

Is it accurate to say that just as a tree needs its roots to thrive, so too does a human need to be rooted in a belief system that consistently informs his life if he is to succeed to the fullest? Will the disparity between what Daniel believes (atheism) and how he lives (Jesus) ultimately cause Daniel some big problems? I'm not sure. But it seems to me that better stories find their way into our daily lives even if we don't believe them. Indeed, this is precisely the situation with Western society.

Historian Tom Holland argues that "people in the West, even those who may imagine that they have emancipated themselves from Christian belief, in fact, are shot through with Christian assumptions about almost everything. ...All of us in the West are goldfish, and the water that we swim in is Christianity."[30]

My friend is drawn to Christian people and appreciates Christian values because he is more Christian than he knows. The Jesus story has woven itself into the very fabric of Western existence, because that's what better stories do.

This truth comes at me hard and helps me kick down a few bars of my mortal cage. Not only are some stories better than others, but the better story, even though broadly rejected, lingers on, shaping the lives of those most viscously opposed to it. Tom Holland brings the point to life through his reflections on the "We Are the World" benefit concert, where dozens of rock stars came together to feed starving Africans in the mid-80s:

> Musicians who had spent their careers variously bedding groupies and snorting coke off trays balanced on the heads of dwarves played sets in aid of the starving....That charity should be offered to the needy and that a stranger in a foreign land was no less a brother or sister than was a next-door neighbour were principles that had always been fundamental to the Christian message.[31]

Try as we might in the Western world, we don't seem able to escape the Christian message. We keep embracing its founding principles long after we have forgotten the specific stories and rejected the theology. It is both shocking and comforting to realize that most of the people who prefer the confines of the mortal cage have the fingerprints of Jesus stamped all over them! This discovery shores up my confidence that there is a greater truth in the Jesus story still worth listening to.

End Notes:

[30] See https://www.churchtimes.co.uk/articles/2019/27-september/features/features/tom-holland-interview-we-swim-in-christian-waters

[31] Tom Holland, *Dominion*, (New York: Basic Books, 2019), 497-498.

Chapter 12

What does your heart long for? Listen to that

> *Suppose this black pit of a kingdom of yours is the only world. Well, it strikes me as a pretty poor one... [We can make] a play-world which licks your real world hollow. That's why I'm going to stand by the play-world. I'm on Aslan's side even if there isn't any Aslan to lead it!*
> C.S. Lewis

"Is everything okay in here?" That's how we met Mark—peeking in our front door after noticing smoke and lots of commotion as he walked by. Something had gotten a little too close to the stove, resulting in some hysterics, but we managed to avoid burning down the house. After our inauspicious intro, Mark and I became friends. It wasn't long before he and his wife and daughter were coming to our community barbecues and eventually our "food and philosophy" nights.

Mark quickly brought up many thoughtful objections to the Christian faith early in our friendship. It was simply a false story to him, and he had plenty of reasons and proofs for its easy dismissal. But the more I listened, the more I realized that the objections were not from angst about historical inaccuracy or factual truth claims. His complaint was deeper: it came from the gut. It was not that Mark felt Christianity couldn't be true; he did not *want* it to be true. Mark had embraced an entirely different story. Instead of subscribing to the ancient Christian tale of "I believe in God Almighty, creator of heaven and earth," he preferred the story, "I believe in myself, the measure of all things, master of my own destiny."[32] This is the dominant story of our time, the one people want to believe. In my experience, there is no arguing a person out of it. The blunt "Here are ten really good reasons to believe in God", approach falls on deaf ears. The stories that shape us come from a much deeper place than mere fact and reason. So instead of arguing with Mark and his family, we invited them into our lives. If the story of divine love is better, I figured it would become evident through observation, not argumentation.

"What did we do to deserve such unconditional love?" Mark said one day after an impromptu conversation about God's divine rescue story with a few of my friends. I could tell that Mark was starting to see how his deep human need to be accepted despite imperfection might be better met in a different story than the one he preferred.

The heart of every worldview story is faith (not facts), and the blood that pumps through that heart is desire. The question of belief is answered through our affections more than our reasons, through our longings more than our knowledge of the truth. At the end of the day, we do not embrace the worldview that has most thoroughly convinced our intellect. We welcome the worldview we want to be true. In Aldous Huxley's book *Ends and Means* he describes the primacy of desire when it comes to faith and worldview with refreshing, albeit troubling, candour:

> I had motives for not wanting the world to have a meaning, and consequently assumed that it had none. I was able without any difficulty to find satisfying reasons for this assumption. The philosopher who finds no meaning in the world is not concerned exclusively with a problem in pure metaphysics. He is also concerned to prove that there is no valid reason why he personally should not do as he wants to do. For myself, as no doubt for most of my friends, the philosophy of meaninglessness was essentially an instrument of liberation from a certain system of morality. We objected to the morality because it interfered with our sexual freedom. The supporters of this system claimed that it embodied the meaning—the Christian meaning, they insisted—of the world. There was one admirably simple method of confuting these people and justifying ourselves in our erotic revolt: we would deny that the world had any meaning whatever.[33]

Huxley desired sexual freedom, so he built an entire philosophical system to justify fulfilling those desires. That's what humans do. As Christian author Alan Hirsch says, reason is always in the employment of love.[34] Our hearts tell us what we want, and our minds do whatever is necessary to make it happen. We all feel our way into belief first. Reasons are important too, but they always come later.

New York University professor of philosophy and law Thomas Nagel also betrays his allegiance to his affections: "I want atheism to be true...It isn't just that I don't believe in God...I don't want there to be a God; I don't want the universe to be like that."[35]

C.S. Lewis revealed the same depth of desire, reflecting upon his pre-Christian state: "I had always wanted, above all things, not to be 'interfered with.'"[36]

For me, this realization was a liberating breath of fresh air. My faith goes deeper than reason, and so does everyone else's. C.S. Lewis was on to this long before I was. In his book *The Silver Chair*, Lewis recounts how an evil witch had convinced everyone that the dark underworld was all there was. With her music and magical charms, conveyed through a glowing fire, everyone had become stupefied into thinking that there was nothing more to life than caves, damp air, and blackness. Suddenly, Puddleglum—the pessimistic, Eeyore-like protagonist of the story—wakes from his stupor; as he listens keenly to the witch's version of reality, he decides it is not worth believing, even if it is true. The deep longings of his heart pull him to turn his back even on the obvious material reality that surrounds him. He breaks the spell by stomping out the hypnotic fire and defying the queen with these words:

> But there's one more thing to be said, even so. Suppose we have only dreamed or made up all those things—trees and grass and sun and moon and stars and Aslan himself. Suppose we have. Then all I can say is that, in that case, the made-up things seem a good deal more important than the real ones. Suppose this black pit of a kingdom of yours is the only world. Well, it strikes me as a pretty poor one. And that's a funny thing when you come to think of it. We're just babies making

up a game, if you're right. But four babies playing a game can make a play-world which licks your real world hollow. That's why I'm going to stand by the play-world. I'm on Aslan's side even if there isn't any Aslan to lead it![37]

When this doubt-filled, doomsday, "we are all gonna die", character looks inward, he feels the deep longings of his heart—and acts on them. When he does, his misgivings and bleak outlook on life take a back seat to a more profound truth that emerges from within.

Of all the stories that exist to shape us, which one connects most beautifully with the deep longings of our hearts? That is the critical question. It is precisely this point that unchained Dostoevsky from the tyranny of his doubt-filled life.

> God gives me sometimes moments of perfect peace; in such moments I love and believe that I am loved; in such moments I have formulated my creed, wherein all is clear and holy to me. This creed is extremely simple; here it is: I believe that there is nothing lovelier, deeper, more sympathetic, more rational, more manly, and more perfect than the Saviour; I say to myself with jealous love that not only is there no one else like Him, but that there could be no one. I would even say more: If anyone could prove to me that Christ is outside the truth, and if the truth really did exclude Christ, I should prefer to stay with Christ and not with truth.[38]

Like Puddleglum, Dostoevsky saw in clear moments something so wholly desirable in Jesus that strict reasoning and argumentation became secondary considerations. So it is for all of humanity. Monk, theologian, and activist Thomas Merton offered this prayer for those of us who live under the shadow of doubt's mountain and who, despite all the darkness, still long for something better.

> My Lord God, I have no idea where I am going. I do not see the road ahead of me. I cannot know for certain where it will end. Nor do I really know myself, and the fact that I think that I am following your will does not mean that I am actually doing so. But I believe that the desire to please you does, in fact, please you.[39]

If desire really is at the blazing centre of everything that shapes human life, how can we be sure that our desires are correct? Most people I know, myself included, seem to have desires more aligned with Huxley than Jesus. Lesser stories have a habit of being very compelling, especially in moments of fleshly weakness. As Canadian philospher James K. A. Smith notes in his book *On the Road with Augustine*, "The human heart is never satisfied with anything finite but that never stops us from trying!"[40]

Even still, buried beneath these strong but superficial desires, humans across history have demonstrated a longing for something more, something beyond ourselves. This is why spirituality and religion will never die out. Smith believes that the feeling of "not at-homeness" that so many experience in this world is a postcard from God read by our hearts. Our deep inner longings move us in the direction of divine love if we have the ears to listen. The better story offered by Christ prevails because it speaks to the greater aches of our being.

The lesser stories we desire and to which we give ourselves always come up short. In a public debate noted atheist Christopher Hitchens was once asked what the purpose of life was. "Sex," he answered. "It is wonderful, but it does have diminishing returns." The lesser stories we grab hold of are all vain attempts to obtain what finite pleasures can't achieve, as the famous quote, "A man knocking on the door of a brothel is knocking for God," so aptly suggests.[41]

Reason is important. But reason is not the engine that drives the spiritual truck. In the struggle for faith, "What do I long for?" will always be a better question than, "What do I know?"

If ever there was a story where deep longing produced unlikely faith, it's my friend Derrin's. He heard the news: a new family was moving into his apartment building. He was excited. In his estimation, the apartment needed more kids, and I had four. But Derrin's excitement became muted when he learned that his new neighbour was the pastor of a local church. This was not good news at all! As a gay man, Derrin was sure my family had made a wrong choice moving into a building with such a high percentage of gay residents. He just hoped things wouldn't get ugly.

Derrin grew up in Saskatchewan in the '80s. Even as a young boy, he knew something was different about himself, but he had no understanding or concept of what it could be. When the topic of "gay" came up in his conservative prairie province, it was always in the context of hate. He heard a constant refrain that gay people should be quarantined because they were pedophiles or deviant monsters. Derrin had no one to talk to about his sexuality. Insecurity and low self-esteem flooded his life until he began to entertain serious thoughts of suicide. Getting out of the Canadian Midwest and discovering the gay community in the larger urban areas of Canada was salvation for Derrin. He learned that many were like him—he wasn't a freak after all. With the support and acceptance of his community, his confidence grew. In response to the trauma he experienced growing up gay, Derrin developed what he called a "fuck you" attitude towards religion. Sadly, along with his anger response, he also developed an alcohol addiction. As he sought help, even Alcoholics Anonymous was too Christian for him. "There is no way a Christian-based organization can help me," he thought.

To build a bridge into this man's life seemed unlikely at best. However, Derrin and his partner had a dog—and a problem. They were going on vacation, and their plans for dog care fell through at the last minute. Shortly before their trip Mistin was talking to Derrin and discovered that they were on the verge of cancelling everything because of the dog. She immediately offered: "We will take the dog." This gesture of neighbourliness cracked open the door to the possibility of friendship.

Over time, we began to see each other more. Our little conversations in the hall and parking garage became more regular. Eventually, Derrin and his partner came over for dinner at our house. Then we began participating together in block parties and building get-togethers.

One day, about a year into our friendship, Derrin asked me out for coffee. As we sat and talked, he let me know that the last three years of his life had been filled with difficulty and disappointment. Addiction had brought him low, and through his rehab, he was coming to believe there was something more to life than just this material world. As Derrin began tuning in to his deeper longings, he felt increasingly uncomfortable in his mortal cage. Perhaps there was a God? He wanted to know if we might explore this together.

"Sure," I said with a smile. "I am a pastor, after all."

Understandably, he wasn't interested in talking about big ideas with me right away. Could I be trusted? Would I ultimately condemn him? Derrin was still convinced the church had nothing but bad news for gay people. So in the early days of our relationship, conversations were slow. I was content to go at his pace.

Another common thread that drew us together was our defective hips. Years of hockey and football had ruined one of mine and degenerative arthritis had wrecked one of his. We both found ourselves needing surgery at the same time. Before we went under the knife, we were a frightful sight. We looked like a couple of mountain gorillas hobbling in and out of our building! As we did rehab together three days a week, our friendship blossomed more than ever. In all this time, now coming up on two years, not once did his being gay come up in our conversations.

One day after our swim, we ate lunch at Derrin's house. Over hot bowls of Derrin's delicious homemade stew, the conversation about Jesus and sexuality finally burst open. It had taken months and months to get to this point. Derrin had many of the same objections and questions about Christianity that plague me. The main grievances he brought up that particular Friday were the problem of evil, the Church's failure, the reliability of Scripture, and Christians saying stupid things. On this last point, the topic of his being gay was finally broached. Franklin Graham's name came up. According to this Christian leader, Derrin's gayness was somehow responsible for Hurricane Katrina and every other natural catastrophe. "Fuck Graham," spat my friend.

I quickly realized there was no point in attempting to answer every objection to the Christian faith, and I certainly wasn't going to defend stupidity. For Derrin, venting that day was a therapeutic mechanism for all the hurt and disenfranchisement he'd felt throughout his life. Honestly, I found myself agreeing with most of his objections! I told Derrin that Jesus' number one criticism while on the earth was towards the foolishness of religious leaders, so we were in good company when we both expressed frustrations over the foolish things religious people say in our day.

After one conversation, Derrin told me, "You know, Dennis, I just believe there has got to be more to this world. So much has happened to me that can't be a blind coincidence, like you moving into this building at exactly this time that I'm searching for more. That's crazy!"

"I like to call it divine providence," I said with a smile. "It's a much better story than random chance."

"Yeah, divine providence," he said.

Eventually, we moved out of that apartment, which was a real test for my new hip. It was Monday afternoon, and I told my kids we were taking a break from unpacking and going for a walk. I took a step towards the door and fell over. Pain knifed through the upper portion of my left thigh. This was no cramp. I could not walk! The pain did not let up, and I needed to go to the ER. Had all this hard work of moving compromised my hip replacement? Fear filled my mind. I sent a group text asking several friends to pray, including Derrin. He called me immediately, telling me he was coming to take me to the ER.

As he helped me into the car, he said, "I'm not just taking you to the hospital for your benefit. I need to talk to you." As we limped into the crowded emergency room, it became evident that we would have plenty of time to talk! And so we did—for the next three hours.

The day before, Derrin, who had been attending our church for a couple of months, had shocked us all by coming forward to take communion. He told me how he had not planned to take communion on Sunday and even resented my appeal to embrace faith "today" at the communion table. But as the music played, he experienced an inexplicable compulsion to come forward and receive communion as an act of faith. He experienced an inescapable longing to be loved by God, to belong, and to matter in ways that transcend the usual means of gaining self-worth: wealth, image, and power. To his surprise, he obeyed the prompting and took communion.

"What does this mean?" he asked. "I have had no dramatic experience of Jesus. There has been no bolt of lightning for me. What is happening?"

I spoke of faith growing first as a longing in our hearts that we can't ignore. Over our many hours together that night, Derrin again brought up numerous questions and potential impediments to his belief in the Christian story. But it seemed that his desire had shifted, and the animus towards the Christian faith that I sensed early on in our friendship had been replaced with an affectionate curiosity. The love, grace, hope, and belonging of the Christian story he had been experiencing through our family and our little church community had altered his perspective. But still, he seemed far from a full embrace of God's grand rescue story for humanity.

Naturally, the elephant in the room was the question of his being gay. Through our years together, he repeatedly brought up how evangelical Christians blamed natural disasters on the gays and how churches like Westboro Baptist make Christianity impossible for him. In these instances, I could only shake my head and agree with him. Hate-filled natural disaster blaming has no place in Jesus' better story. My repudiation of his needless suffering at the hands of angry people who claimed to be Christians seemed enough for him. Until this point, he had never actually asked me what the Scripture teaches about homosexuality or my personal views on the subject. It was enough for him to know that I loved him as he was.

We finally arrived home around midnight. I asked him if we might pray together as another "step of newfound faith." He agreed, and we talked to God. It was a beautiful, sincere, unscripted reach heavenward.

Months later the phone call came. An evangelical organization wanted me to do a breakout session at their conference on "discipling those gay people." The whole tone of the conversation didn't sit well with me, so I told them I was not interested. But as I thought about it, an idea occurred to me. Instead of giving a speech about how I help gay people in their faith, what if I brought Derrin to the conference so we could have a conversation in front of everyone about discipleship? I thought it would be much better to talk *with* a gay person than *about* a gay person. I asked Derrin, who looked at me like I was crazy—but he couldn't escape the idea either, and eventually he agreed to help me. Over three months, we put our shared story together and titled the conversation "Loving Beyond Labels." In this lead-up to our talk, we finally got into what the Bible says and my personal views.

By this time, our commitment to each other's well-being was so strong that this conversation wasn't as big a deal as it would have been had it come earlier. Derrin wanted the straight goods on what the Bible said about him as a gay man. I showed him the six verses that condemn homosexuality and the many verses that support heterosexual marriage. I presented him with the two competing views within Christianity regarding homosexuality: one represented by gay Christian writer and leader Matthew Vines, who supports monogamous homosexual marriage, and the other by gay Christian writer and leader Christopher Yuan, who supports abstinence as the only option for gay Christians. Understandably, Derrin liked Mathew Vines' point of view, but he also had no problem with Christopher's stance, as long as it wasn't forced upon him.

Derrin admitted that for him the better story would be to embrace Vines' view. Accepting it would remove the tension he felt between being gay and his growing desire to be a Christian. He followed this up by admitting that just because something is easier doesn't mean it's right. Our commitment to love each other remained strong through all of our tough conversations. This kind of love is at the heart of the better story. As we put our co-presentation together, we jotted down the difficult questions which would inevitably come:

1. If Christianity teaches that marriage is between a man and a woman, what sacrifices might Derrin be expected to make with his partner of 18 years if he moved forward into the Christian faith?

2. As Derrin continues to explore his faith and is increasingly involved in the life of the church, should his role be

limited because of his gay relationship? To what extent? If so, what is his motivation to stay involved?

3. If Christians can relax the traditional rules on divorce and women's roles in the church, why not on same-sex attraction? Is there legitimately some interpretive flexibility here?

4. If Dennis remains committed to the traditional view of marriage and Derrin remains committed to his lifestyle, what will come of this relationship? Is a compromise possible?

After an hour of sharing our stories, we asked these questions in a jam-packed room at the conference. No concrete answers were offered, but what we received from the crowd of Christian men and women was far better than any policy solutions. Derrin received a standing ovation for his courage to speak to Christians seeking a better way forward amid complicated and controversial issues around human sexuality. The compassion of that capacity crowd clapping and cheering did more for Derrin's spiritual growth than any breakthrough policy conversation on "what to do about those gays" ever could.

Our friendship held firm, and Derrin and his partner became like uncles to our kids. We trusted each other because compassionate love was at the centre of our relationship, not policy and positions. Sadly, in the fall of 2019, Derrin relapsed into alcoholism and tragically slipped from this world. The hole that his unexpected departure caused is still felt to this day.

My entire friendship with Derrin and its attendant journey into faith would have never been possible if our church had had a policy about gay people. The better story is the one that, at its core, demands a genuine love for other people regardless of the complexities of their lives. The Christian story contains a depth of other-oriented love that no other story surpasses. Yes, this love sometimes gets buried under Christian politics, dogma, and fear. But transcendent love and belonging is the message that Jesus brings to humankind. This is precisely what our hearts long for even when we don't realize it. The Jesus story and the deep longing of our hearts were meant to fit together, and this is what pulled Derrin out of his mortal cage and into hope in God, despite mountains of obstacles that stood in the way.

End Notes:

[32] Robert E. Webber, *The Divine Embrace* (Grand Rapids, Mich.: Baker Books),105.

[33] Aldous Huxley, *End of Means* (New York: Harper & Brothers Publishers, 1937), 269-273.

[34] Alan and Debra Hirsch, *Untamed* (Grand Rapids, Mich.: Baker Books, 2010), 55.

[35] Thomas Nagel, *The Last Word* (Oxford: Oxford University Press, 1997),130-131.

[36] C.S. Lewis, *Surprised by Joy* (Orlando, Florida: Harcourt Inc, 1955), 228.

[37] C.S. Lewis, *The Silver Chair* (New York: Harper Trophy, 1953),182.

[38] Letter To Mme. N. D. Fonvisin (1854), as published in *Letters of Fyodor Michailovitch Dostoevsky to his Family and Friends* (1914), translated by Ethel Golburn Mayne, Letter XXI, 71.

[39] Thomas Merton, *Thoughts In Solitude* (New York: Farrar, Straus and Giroux, 1997), 79.

[40] James K.A. Smith, *On the Road with Saint Augustine* (Ada Mich.: Brazos Press, 2019), 13.

[41] Variously ascribed to Chesterton, St. Francis, and St. Augustine, we have discovered that the only documented source of this quotation is the book *The World, The Flesh, and Father Smith* by Bruce Marshall (1945). And the quote is really: ". . .the young man who rings the bell at the brothel is unconsciously looking for God." (p. 108) see https://www.chesterton.org/other-quotations/

Chapter 13

Certainty is overrated

I am beginning to believe that nothing is quite so uncertain as facts.
Edward Curtis

My grand intellectual efforts to achieve theological certainty are what made the bars of my mortal cage all the thicker. Of course, attempts to protect and preserve one's faith are entirely understandable. We naturally safeguard what is precious to us. Helicopter moms and gated communities exist for good reasons. It's just that sometimes overprotection can be more of a problem than its opposite. This has turned out to be the case for me and my troubled faith. Faith is not correct thinking about God or the Bible; it is trusting in God. Faith is not about the specifics of what we believe but about whom we trust. Of course, Christian people believe in some specific ideas about God and reject others. Having actual content to one's belief is not the problem. The problem is a preoccupation with being correct in every detail about that belief. Fastidious attempts to dot every theological 'i' and cross every exegetical 't' can be a major, though well-intentioned, cause for Christian disillusionment.

Faith based on knowing something correctly has undeniable benefits. It creates clear lines of demarcation that allow people to know who is in and who is out. Dividing lines are beneficial in creating a sense of belonging. Additionally, focusing one's faith on correct thinking provides a sense of certainty. Certainty creates stability, something we all long for in such an unstable world. Some may feel that a faith that distances itself from certainty is no faith at all; what good is a faith that doesn't produce belonging and stability?

But there is a serious downside when we cling to our need to get the details of our faith *just right*. When we fear losing the stability and belonging that come with certainty, we can find ourselves becoming militantly preoccupied with correct thinking in every area of life. Suddenly, it becomes critical that we can defend, at all costs, certain familiar beliefs and practices. This preoccupation with correct thinking is a significant factor behind the bloody infighting that we find throughout Christian history, as well as many of the countless church splits and various divisions within the faith today.

As an extreme—and even comical—example, consider Wilfrid, a seventh-century Northumbrian monk and powerful church influencer in Britain. When he visited Ireland, he freaked out that the monks there didn't have the proper hairstyles, nor did they follow the correct calendar of holy days. This was no slight divergence from the more perfect way. Wilfrid had been to Rome, and he had seen the light. Any Irishman who objected to his changes faced strict life-upending penalties and received the callous reminder of where the Irish belonged in the hierarchy of Christianity. Compared to Rome, distant Ireland was but a "pimple on the chin of the earth!"[42] Irish Christians needed to know their place. Religious certainty had made its way into the barber's chair! This sounds laughable, but I remember growing up in my fundamentalist church and hearing sermons on how important it was for *godly* boys to make sure their hair was cut clear over the ears, short on top and tapered in the back.

This point becomes clearer if we look at it in terms of a more familiar relationship: marriage. A successful marriage is not determined by confidently held knowledge of one's spouse. Successful marriages are built on trusting each other and pursuing one another, whether or not we understand each other correctly.[43] The same is true with God. Trust and pursuit matter far more than making sure one's theology is precisely correct by some standard or dogma. In the world of faith, it is okay to let go of the need to be correct. Trust doesn't claim to know everything for certain. In defending the Bible so rigorously, in fighting for our proper understanding of God, we have missed the opportunity to trust and pursue God, which is the whole point of faith.

At age 34, author and Duke divinity professor Kate Bowler was struck with stage 4 cancer. As she was coming to grips with her mortality, she wrote an article about her struggle with the disease for the *New York Times*. It was a raw and uncut look at how faith and suffering mix. The article was full of uncertainty and wrestling. It became immensely popular. Mountains of mail soon covered Bowler's desk. Unfortunately, many of these letters came brimming full of reasons, explanations, and trite cliches intended to help her understand her suffering and provide certainty for the reasons behind her dark trial. As she recounts in her book *Everything Happens for a Reason and Other Lies I've Loved*, most of them did not help. Here is a taste of the "advice" she received:

- A Hindu writer said, "We have had many millions of births and deaths in different life-forms, so don't worry. This life shall pass, and your soul will move forward to its next step."

- A Christian neighbour blurted out in the midst of some of the more gruesome parts of living with cancer, "Everything happens for a reason; there is some important Divine plan in all of this. God is good all the time."

- A secularist wrote, "I find it comforting to believe the universe is random; then the God I might believe in could no longer be cruel."

- A "power of positive thinking" guru promised that healing was possible by chiming in, "Your attitude determines your destiny."

- A reformed pastor wrote: "God is a just God to let you die; these are the consequences of your sin."

- A medical professional coldly gives advice, "The sooner you get used to the idea of dying, the better."[44]

Bowler understands that to be human is to ask, "Why?" We want to fully understand why things happen to us. Sure answers to the *why* questions are a great comfort. Bowler muses that some things like tragedy lie beyond the reach of good reasons and should, therefore, remain untouched by them. If the search for logic amid chaos is a fruitless one, what then?

Bowler suggests that we give up on the illusion of control and certainty. Before her illness, Bowler wrote the world's first history of the prosperity gospel movement. The entire movement hinges on the twin jewels of control and certainty. If you ascribe to certain spiritual laws and beliefs about God, backed up with appropriate Bible verses, you can control your destiny and be sure to avoid pain and suffering on earth. The more you believe in and adhere to these laws, the more control and certainty you have in your life. Of course, all of this is bogus. Still, as Bowler expanded her search beyond the prosperity gospel, she discovered that the tendency to build systems of belief and practice that desperately reach for control and certainty is universal. Bowler has rightly come to realize that all such reaching ends in despair. She concludes that a much better way to live is the practice of surrendering to the will of God.[45]

She is quick to admit that she is not very good at it. None of us are; control is what we all desire. Embracing mystery and uncertainty in faith is frightening business. But, as biblical scholar and theologian Peter Enns says, trusting God with childlike faith regardless of how confident we feel takes far more courage than knowing something for certain.[46] Developing the courage to trust amid uncertainties is the better way.

Jesuit philosopher John Kavanaugh learned precisely this lesson from Mother Teresa. His struggles and doubts had put him on a pilgrimage to India to seek her out. As this troubled soul faced the mighty matriarch of Christian charity, he asked of her one thing: "Pray that I have clarity."

"No, I will not do that," Mother Theresa immediately replied. Surprised, Kavanaugh asked her why.

"Clarity is the last thing you are clinging to, and you must learn to let go of it," she said. The explanation flummoxed the weary traveller.

"But you always seem to have clarity," he responded.

Mother Teresa chuckled. "I have never had clarity in my life. What I have is trust, so I will pray that you trust God."[47]

Mystery allows for trust far more than certainty does. I am learning that the bonds of my mortal cage loosen a little when I say things like, "I don't know, but I'm trusting God", rather than trying to spit out concrete answers, dogma, or proof texts supporting a rigid adherence to a list of beliefs.

End Notes:

[42] Peter Brown, *The Rise of Western Christendom*, (Chichester, West Sussex: Wiley-Blackwell 2013), 360-362.

[43] Peter Enns, *The Sin of Certainty* (Newark, NJ: Audible, 2016), Chapter 1 35:41.

[44] Kate Bowler, *Everything Happens for a Reason and Other Lies I've Loved* (New York: Random House, 2018), 112-114.

[45] Ibid., Chapter 2.

[46] Enns, *The Sin of Certainty*, 15.

[47] Ibid., Chap 7 4:22:37.

Chapter 14

Modern Apologetics Can Become an Adventure in Missing the Point

A person who is not an artist cannot be a Christian
William Blake

In a scene from the Jim Candy and Steve Martin classic, *Plains Trains and Automobiles,* the two lead actors are driving on the wrong side of the highway. They have no idea that they are heading into oncoming traffic. A concerned driver gets up to speed with them and begins yelling frantically across the median, "You're going the wrong way!" Candy mocks the warning, yelling and gesturing at the couple trying to help him. Martin finally sticks his head out the window to try to hear exactly what they are so desperately attempting to communicate. He gets the message and turns to Candy. "They said we are going the wrong way," he blurts, confused. Candy is sure now that they are drunk; he rolls his eyes and asks, "How would they know where we are going?" A second later, in a moment of brilliantly filmed panic, they both look up to see two semi-trucks coming straight for them, side by side. The semis zoom by either side of their car, knocking off the side mirrors and sending up sparks.

When I see Christians relentlessly pursuing facts, reason, and certainty as the fundamental necessities of the Christian faith, I empathize with that other driver. I want to yell, just like in the movie, "You are going the wrong way!" The twin semis of self-righteousness and disillusionment are coming, and they can do fearsome damage.

Christianity didn't achieve its unprecedented success because every detail of the New Testament could be proven with clinical certainty or because archaeological evidence for Old Testament stories was finally and incontrovertibly uncovered. Ancient believers did not even remotely consider the "truth" of the Bible in any modern, evidence-based sense. For at least the first 1,000 years of Christian history, the primary interpretive method for the Bible among Western Christians was allegorical. Take Pope Gregory I (540-604), for example. He told the Christians of his day that the Bible was a great encoded message sent by God to "cast fire into the heart." Its pages, he said, echoed with the mighty whisper of God. It was for this "whisper" that the devout Christian should listen, reading the Bible "between the lines"—paying less attention to the factual details of the text itself than to a message from God that lay behind the text.[48] Augustine, in his magisterial autobiography, *Confessions*, wrote, "What harm is there if a reader believes what you, the Light of all truthful minds, show him to be the true meaning? It may not even be the meaning which the writer had in mind."[49]

I'm not suggesting the Christian faith isn't a historical one. The apostles certainly had enough confidence to launch a movement based on an actual Jesus who did extraordinary things, was killed, and then raised from the dead. But the earliest Christians were captured more by the implications of the story, not by the gritty details of it. The gospel accounts are not air-tight, Sherlock Holmes-calibre investigations; they are patchy eyewitness accounts intended to bolster confidence in God's great rescue story. It was the wonder of what God had done through Jesus that filled the Roman world with hope and joy, and led to such an incredible conversion rate. What people talked about was the unimaginable love of God in Christ. Eventually, over time, converts began to wonder precisely how God's son had come to the earth. Wonder itself led to wondering. The "what" question faded into the background of the Christian story, and people began attempting to answer the less important but more divisive question of "how" this all came to be.

This steady movement from the general to the specific spelled trouble for Christianity. Major controversies erupted as different conclusions to the "how" of God's story overtook people's thoughts. The joy and unity found at the foot of the cross dissolved into bitter disagreements over highly technical theological issues. Splits and fighting became the norm, leading to wars and bloodshed.

One example of the countless divisions and difficulties of early Christianity came in the fifth century as the church debated the "official" position on the nature of Jesus. Did Jesus have one nature or two? The correct answer, according to the divines at Chalcedon, was two. Jesus was 100% human in nature and 100% divine in nature. They explained that if Jesus had only one nature, he could neither be truly divine nor human, making for a lousy Saviour. Not everyone was convinced. Another group, the Monophysites (literally "one nature") weren't buying it at all. To them, it was absurd to say someone had two natures. They saw it as unhelpful nonsense to categorize Jesus as having anything other than a single nature. Of course, both groups loved and worshiped Jesus, and attempted to shape their existence around his beautiful life, but the points of commonality had to be pushed aside because of the differences between them. Eventually, the Monophysites were so severely persecuted that they welcomed the Islamic invasion of their territories in the 600s![50]

The divisiveness of Christianity only continued as differences between the eastern and western versions of the Christian story were expanded, debated, and exploited. With the coming of the Reformation in the 16th century, irreparable cracks spread across Christendom like the spider fractures that spread across a frozen pond when struck with a large stone.

Eventually, after centuries of in-fighting, the church was sufficiently fragmented for yet another great movement that would push Christianity to the margins. Instead of answering the "how" of the Christian story, the Enlightenment brought a new question to the forefront of Western culture: Is the Christian story even true at all? The great doubters of the 18th through 20th centuries had to be answered decisively.

But the world's way of knowing had shifted. After the influence of philosophers like Rene Descartes, the truth could only be captured through logic and, eventually, science. Empirical proof became the principal factor for legitimacy. Christians, like everyone else, are products of their era, so they played along with these new rules. Experts emerged and began to rebuild the Christian story along strict lines of physical, textual, and historical evidence.

This trend continues unabated into our day. Faith has been reduced to fact checking. Adherence to a series of historical facts and signing on to attendant dogmas that flow from those details is all that matters. Books like *The Case for Christ, Evidence Demands a Verdict, The Reason for God, Total Truth* and hosts of others fill up our bookshelves with rational arguments for God. Conferences and speakers specializing in proving the historicity and accuracy of the actual story are a top priority.

Even multimillion-dollar museums have been constructed to prove the accuracy of historical details about Biblical events like a worldwide flood, the people of Israel crossing the Red Sea, and Jonah being swallowed by a whale. Fear is the mindset behind these efforts. If Christianity is to survive, then all the benefits of the better story must be put on hold until the precise details of its record can be proven beyond a reasonable doubt within a highly technical, modernistic system.

Herein lies a significant problem: the Christian story was never intended to be ripped up into little pieces and studied the way a mortician studies a cadaver. When Christianity bowed its knee to the man in the white lab coat and submitted its story to the unforgiving scrutiny of science, the splendour of the good news was lost. We all have a story that gives direction to our lives. The big stories upon which we hitch our wagons exist beyond the scope of anything fully provable. Of course, it is not a waste of time to shore up confidence in a story by sifting through various kinds of evidence for its authenticity. I've read all the books I've mentioned above and many more besides, and some have been very helpful. But in the end, faith in one story or another exists in all of us irrespective of evidence. Sadly, Christians, myself among them, have become masters at missing the beauty of the forest for the trees. We have spent our time taking apart the story to answer questions that were never meant to be asked. We've bent over backwards to prove incidental details about the story, and in the process, we've become like the comedian who has to explain his own jokes. Lasting faith must be formed and rooted at a much deeper level than simply being convinced by the relatively low distortion rates between Alexandrian and Byzantine text types or understanding precisely how the Jericho walls managed to fall.

As early as the 18th century, poet William Blake lamented that Christians, by and large, had embraced this scientific vision of faith with its rational theologies, evidentialist apologetics, and reductionist Bible readings.[51] Faith held in bondage to the technician and the critical historian is no faith at all, according to Blake. It was anathema for him to bind faith so tightly with facts. As he said, "Science dismisses the inner life, and closes off the imagination.... Human reason and modern science make us both more powerful and less alive at the same time.... A person who is not an artist cannot be a Christian." Blake was pushing Christians back towards the inner imaginative side of our being. "God cannot be grasped through calculation," he said, "only vision."[52]

More recently, literary critic Northrop Frye, like Blake, has resisted the urge to make faith all about factual legitimacy. Jesus dropped into our world as a counter-historical figure from another dimension; his presence and unfolding story upended all norms and paradigms and changed the world forever. The transforming presence and work of Jesus is the big idea into which Christians place their hope. "Searching in the nooks and crannies of the gospel text for a credibly historical Jesus is merely one more excuse for despising and rejecting him," Frye wrote.[53]

James K. A. Smith on page 51 and 52 of his book *How Not To Be Secular*, further adds to the conversation by criticizing the "industry" of Christian philosophy and apologetics today as "already conceding the game to exclusive humanism by playing on their turf." The story of God coming to redeem humanity in the person of Jesus exists to capture our imagination and shape the direction of our lives. The account exists not so that we can prove it true in a scientific, technical, literal, or even a strictly historical sense. To chain faith to science is a costly adventure in missing the point.

Finally, author and educator James Turner helps us see this point a bit more clearly:

> In trying to adapt their religious beliefs to socioeconomic change, to new moral challenges, to novel problems of knowledge, to the tightening standards of science, the defenders of God slowly strangled Him...unbelief emerged because church leaders too often forgot the transcendence essential to any worthwhile God....they tried to bring God in line with modernity.[54]

It was a strangulation of God by the rope of good intentions. I was God's executioner, but quite by accident! I had been trying to fit God into a purely modern, scientific, rational box to understand him better myself and explain him to others in a convincing evangelistic fashion. But God does not fit into the boxes we make for him. I know that now, but for a while, when God did not add up to my modernistic expectations, I felt as though I would be locked away in my mortal cage forever. It was only when I realized my unhealthy emphasis on proving God true that I found a way to slip the bars.

End Notes:

[48] Peter Brown, *The Rise of Western Christendom* (Chichester, West Sussex: Wiley-Blackwell, 2013), 204.

[49] Augustine, *Confessions*, 296.

[50] Brown, *The Rise of Western Christendom*, 279-282.

[51] Robert Inchausti, *Subversive Orthodoxy*, (Grand Rapids Mich.: Brazos Press, 2005), 21.

[52] Ibid., 25-27.

[53] Ibid.,148.

[54] James Emery White, *The Rise of the Nones*, (Grand Rapids Mich.: Baker Books, 2014), 52.

Chapter 15

Overcoming Biblical Attachment Disorder (B.A.D.)

Adjust your expectations on what the Bible can deliver...The Bible is an ancient book that simply cannot be dropped on our laps without a lot of thought and wisdom. The Bible is a book to be pondered, thought through, tried out, assessed and argued with; all of these interactions with our holy book are expressions of a trusting but uncertain faith.

Peter Enns

The Bible is both wonderful and terrible, glorious and troubling. I was raised as a Christian to defend the Bible to the very last. Every controversial passage must have a good explanation. If there wasn't one, it was my duty to reserve negative judgment indefinitely until one could be produced. It was drilled into me from a young age that the Bible was God's perfectly preserved word without error. For the first 20 years of my life, I was even taught that this perfectly preserved word was only found in the 1611 King James Version of the Bible; all other versions were from the devil! Mercifully, I navigated beyond this narrow perspective, but it came at a high cost.

I was young and in love. We had met at a wedding. There was an instant connection. I couldn't believe my good fortune. Not only was she absolutely beautiful, but she also was a committed follower of Jesus. She had wit and humour, the voice of an angel, and a captivating personality. It is safe to say I was utterly smitten. We lived far from each other, so our time together was short, but I was undaunted; I commenced writing the moment I returned home. Great hope swelled in me. She was the angel from Edmonton, and she would be mine! Letters quickly turned into phone calls. We talked about everything. It seemed like we fit perfectly together, but then the infamous conversation happened.

"Dennis, what do you think about the Bible?" she asked one day.

"Oh, I love the Bible; it's God's Word; it's our guide. I'm a big fan," I answered, confident.

"Which Bible?" she asked.

"All of them?" I ventured.

There was an alarming pause on the phone.

"What do you think about the King James Bible?"

"Oh, I grew up with the KJV," I assured her. "It's a masterful work if you like Shakespearean English. The King Jimmy is a bit dated and harder to understand, so it wouldn't be my first choice in English translations, but I have no real problems with it."

There was a pause. Clearly, that was the wrong answer. She went on to tell me in no uncertain terms that it would be imperative for me to believe that the KJV was the only inspired word of God for today if our relationship was to continue. I had already moved on from that position, but I wasn't too worried; I had spent a ton of time studying the issue, and I felt like I could help her see things more accurately when it came to the English translation debate.

"Would you be interested in studying this with me?" I asked her. "I have this great book called *The King James Only Controversy* by James White. Let me send you a copy, and then we can work through it together."

"Okay," was her half-hearted reply. I put the phone down, grabbed a copy of the book, and went straight to the post office. A few days later, I got a call from her.

"Hi Dennis, it's me. My dad wants to talk to you."

I cringed.

His appeal was short and precise. "Dennis, if you want to date my daughter, you have to believe that the KJV is God's perfect word for today. You must believe that all the other English versions are corrupt."

I was ready. I tried to talk to him about the minority text and the majority text, about Erasmus, and the history of translation work. He would have none of it.

Finally, in desperation, he said to me. "Dennis, we like you, my daughter likes you, and we think you could be a good husband for her. But can't you just have faith that the KJV is the only inspired word of God for today? Can't you just believe it?"

Place my hope in an English translation—was he serious?

He was dead serious. When I told him that I couldn't do that, it was over just like that. He graciously allowed me to say goodbye to his daughter and passed the phone over to her.

"I can't believe you are dumping me for a king who has been dead for 400 years! You don't owe King James anything!" I managed, before she said goodbye and hung up the phone forever.

Looking back, it is hard to imagine that this episode in my life happened, but it did. It's a bit depressing for me when I realize that pockets of Christians like this still exist worldwide. All of these groups have one thing in common: a commitment to understanding texts of Scripture, or in this case, versions of Scripture, in a certain inflexible way as a vital matter of faith.

Despite my "progressive" view of the KJV, as I moved on with my life, I was still very conscientious about revering the Bible, in most of its English translations, as the very words of God given to us. Each one was precious, each one valuable, each one to be defended and explained in a positive light, no matter how confounding or troubling. Even though I had shed the constraints of the KJV-only position, I still felt that there could be no smudge on the pristine glass of God's Word.

I want to know that God is present. What greater comfort can fulfill that longing than having a flawless holy book I can hold in my hands? All I need are my reading glasses, and I can be ushered into the very presence of God. What devout person *wouldn't* want this to be part of their story? In many ways, this seems to track with what I have said about longing being more important than reason in matters of faith. Shouldn't we follow our hearts on this and "just believe" that we have an inerrant Bible? Granted, most haven't reduced such a belief to a King James only position, but many Christians think similarly to my potential father-in-law about the Bible in general.

Take Al Mohler, president of the Southern Baptist Theological Seminary, for example. He is convinced that the church must have a total commitment to the trustworthiness and truthfulness of the Bible, or else the church is left without a defining authority. Upholding the doctrine of inerrancy is the only way the Bible can be considered trustworthy, so a Christian's philosophy about the Bible must be all-or-nothing. Scripture is the support beam on which Christianity is built. If the Bible is not wholly true and trustworthy, then the support beam for our faith is destroyed, and the whole thing comes crashing down.

Mohler rejects attempts to say that Biblical authority does not require inerrancy:

> "Biblical authority is inescapably impaired if total divine inerrancy is in any way limited or disregarded...I do not allow any line of evidence from outside the Bible to nullify to the slightest degree the truthfulness of any text in all that

the text asserts and proclaims. That statement may appear radical to some readers, but it is the only position that is fully compatible with the claim that every word of Scripture is fully inspired and thus fully true and trustworthy."[55]

Even if one found an error in Scripture large enough to hit Al Mohler in the face and knock him over, he still wouldn't be convinced of its validity because of an *a priori* conviction against that possibility.

I was coming to see that I could no longer stomach the implications and inconsistencies of this position. Decades of Bible study, though helpful in many ways, had created far too many questions in my mind for me to continue to uphold the Bible with the worship-like reverence my upbringing demanded. But could I acknowledge my doubts about the Bible and still be a Christian? Was it truly an all-or-nothing proposition, as Al Mohler suggests? For a long time, I worried that since I could no longer accept a literal, inerrant approach to all of the Bible, I would be forced to choose nothing, landing me back in the cage.

Thankfully, I have since come to see that my approach to the Bible does not have to be either-or.

So how was I to understand the Bible? As I read and studied, I discovered all sorts of buzzwords: infallible, sufficient, inerrant, authoritative, reliable, trustworthy. Which word best described the Bible? As I tried to have some sense of peace about the issue, I was reminded by biblical scholar and former professor at the University of Aberdeen, I. Howard Marshall, that taking any position on the Bible is tricky business indeed:

Should I so much as deviate to the left and suggest that not all the Scripture says is true in the strictest sense of that term, I shall come under strong criticism and possibly even excommunication from the right, not simply for saying so, but for saying so as a confessed evangelical; and should I throw in my lot unreservedly with my colleagues on the right, I shall undoubtedly suffer at the hands of my colleagues on the left, who will doubt not only any claim I dare make to be a biblical scholar but also my sanity.[56]

When I came across problems in the Bible, I was always taught to withhold judgment, read a bit more closely, and do a little more research; if I was patient enough, I would get the correct answer eventually. Genre, context, authorial intent, historical imprecision, or some other plausible explanation would emerge, so that the Scripture's perfect track record could remain. I learned that I could always blame any difficulty on faulty interpretation, and, in a pinch, I could always claim, "In the original autographs, it was perfect."

Marshall believes that we Christians should drop these well-meaning games. Inerrancy, he says, should be abandoned because it "needs so much qualification, even by its defenders, that it is in danger of dying the death of a thousand qualifications."[57] I agree.

New Testament scholar and historian David Bentley Hart aligns with Marshall's thinking.

All Christians believe that the New Testament is divinely inspired; but any coherent account of what this means must involve acknowledgment that God speaks through human beings, in all their historical, cultural, and personal contingency. For those, however, who not only believe that Scripture is inspired, but who are also deeply committed to "literalist," "inerrantist" or "dictational" understandings of inspiration, all the words of the Bible must be understood as direct locutions of God, passing through their human authors like sunlight through the clearest glass, and the canon of the New Testament even though it took a few centuries to concresce into its present form, and has never really existed as anything but a shimmering cloud of countless variants — must be understood as a flawlessly immediate communication, in its every historical and lexical detail, of the teaching of the Holy Spirit and of the faith of the apostolic church. That has never been the only, or even the dominant, Christian understanding of scriptural inspiration. Many modern Christians, in fact, might be quite surprised at the speculative boldness and critical diffidence with which some of the greatest exegetes of Christian late antiquity and the Middle Ages approached the Bible.[58]

As now disgraced author and pastor Bruxy Cavey explains:

Jesus treated the Torah [the first five books of the Old Testament] as God's Word but not God's final word; he himself was God's final word...[Reading], studying, and understanding the Bible is not the goal of a Christ-Follower. Bible knowledge is just a first step toward the goal of following Jesus. Thomas Adams said it best: "The Bible is to us what the star was to the wise men; but if we spend all our time in gazing upon it, observing its motions, and admiring its splendour, without being led to Christ by it, the use of it will be lost on us..." The religious "experts" (those who have dedicated their lives to the academic study of a book) may not be experts in the relationship the Bible points toward...Those who want to follow the way of Jesus must decide whether they will narrowly focus only on the Bible's words as their ultimate authority or let the person of Jesus and the principles that lie behind those words be their guide.[59]

The Bible is like a treasure map that points the way to Jesus. Sadly, I've treated the Bible more like the treasure than the map; it's really easy to do. It is an ancient map: it has some frayed edges, it is smudged in places, and there are some crease marks and unhelpful folds. Sometimes the markings are not as straightforward as we would like, but on the whole, it works. It leads people to Jesus. Jesus is the treasure.

Understanding the Bible as a treasure map has the beneficial effect of shifting the focus away from investigating the technical truths of the Bible to its adequacy for what God intends it to do. This step, according to Marshall, opens up the possibility of "a fresh approach to the Bible which may prove to be illuminating." The Bible becomes a map that "guides people to salvation and the associated way of life."[60] It has taken decades, but this is how I have come to understand the Bible.

I am genuinely thankful for the Bible as my treasure map. As my life has unfolded, it has been easy to see how the map has, time and again, steered me in the right direction. I would be lost without its influence on my life. However, the sharp distinction I am making between treasure and treasure map allows me to take a small step back from the Bible and wrestle more honestly with the conundrums it presents. I'm not forced to aggressively defend genocide passages or bend over backward to synthesize discrepancies in the gospel accounts. The Bible isn't fundamentally a book of history or science. It's not a precise archaeological journal or war archive. It is not a book meant to be authenticated by fact-checkers in every detail, nor is it fundamentally a rule book meant to be obeyed. It's a map that leads to Jesus.

When I content myself to understand the Bible in this way, the dark shadows of doubt that come at me from its pages do not envelope me in quite so dark a hue. My wife loves nothing more than a good hug from me, but if I wrap my arms around her and squeeze for all I am worth, it is not long before the experience goes badly for both of us. When I squeezed the Bible with overzealous affection, I developed Biblical Attachment Disorder, and it nearly got me a life sentence in the mortal cage.

End Notes:

[55] Stanley Gundry, *Five Views on Biblical Inerrancy* (Grand Rapids, Mich.: Zondervan Academic, 2013), 36, 51.

[56] D.A. Carson, *Collected Writing on Scripture* (Wheaton, Illinois: Crossway, 2010), 218.

[57] *Ibid.,* 221.

[58] David Bentley Hart, *The New Testament* (New Haven, Connecticut: Yale University Press), 575.

[59] Bruxy Cavey, *The End of Religion* (Colorado Springs, Colorado: NavPress, 2007) 179, 182,183.

[60] Carson, *Collected Writings on Scripture,* 220.

Chapter 16

The power of a changed life

People, even more than things, have to be restored, renewed, revived, reclaimed, and redeemed; never throw out anyone.
Audrey Hepburn

I hated my dad, pure and simple. He was a colossal failure as a husband and a father. Because of his destructive actions towards our family, he deserved nothing less than my disdain, which is exactly what I gave him. I did not feel guilty for my hatred. I was justified. It would be wrong for me not to hate him.

All this rage was helpful for my football career, and I won many trophies for knocking people over. But other than that single benefit, my hatred caused me all kinds of problems. I got kicked out of school for fighting and was becoming disruptive and rebellious.

All the while, I was blind to the connection between my hatred for my dad and my troubles.

The summer I was 17, I had the chance to go to a Christian camp. It was full of beautiful girls and fun activities, and whatever Bible teaching it might have wouldn't bother me since I had grown up in a church. Two whole weeks in America, far from my home in Canada—and my annoying father. I was in!

I met my counsellor, Marty, on the first day of camp. He was not just interested in hanging out with me, he wanted to help me with my life. In those first couple days, he asked me many questions, including; "How is your relationship with your dad?"

I wasn't expecting that question. I told him straight out: "My Dad? Oh, I hate him. He is a jerk. I wish he were dead."

At that point, all other questions seemed to stop. For the remainder of camp, Marty would keep coming back to this issue.

I thought it was a non-issue. My dad was a jerk, and hating him was the only reasonable response. If it was anyone's issue, it was my dad's. If he would change his ways, I was sure I could forgive him, and perhaps a relationship would be possible.

But that's not how Marty saw it. Since it was a Bible camp, he took me to the Bible.

Over many days, he explained the good news. He told me that the whole story is built around the idea that God loves us, but our misdeeds have created a breach between us and God. God, however, was not content to let us suffer in our ignorance and despair, so divine love became human in the person of Jesus. The divine rescue plan culminated in the death and resurrection of God's son. The death of Jesus frees us from the power of sin (redeems us), and the resurrection of Jesus becomes joy-inducing evidence that even death, the ultimate consequence of sin, is no longer a real threat to us. We, like Jesus, according to the story, can never ultimately die. When the self-sacrificing love of Jesus fills the heart and captures the imagination of those who believe it, a mighty change happens. We can forgive because we have been forgiven. We can love even the unlovable because we were loved when we were unlovable.

I had heard all this before, but I never assumed it could apply to my relationship with my father. It was just kind of churchy stuff, not real-life stuff. In addition to the good news, Marty added some Scriptures that addressed my specific situation. He showed me verses like Ephesians 6:1-2 ("Children, obey your parents...") and Colossians 3:20-21 ("Children, always obey your parents....")

Even though the entire Jesus story was reaching my heart, I still wasn't buying how it might impact my responsibility towards my father. "Not if he's a jerk!" was my angry response.

I felt that if my father wasn't living up to my expectations, I could dishonour him with impunity. According to Marty and the Bible, the better story was highlighting the need for me to honour my father, whether he was worthy or not. I was not fond of that plan at all. This couldn't be a "better story" because it messed with my sense of justice.

Finally, in desperation, I came across a loophole. Both those Bible verses have a warning for dads—fathers are not supposed to provoke their children to anger. My dad had definitely provoked me, so it must be okay for me to hate his guts.

But then Marty took me over to Luke 10:25-37, where I discovered that a person in the Bible had been just like me, looking for a loophole to justify hatred. In the story, a religious leader is asking Jesus for eternal life. He knew he needed to keep the commands of loving God and loving his neighbour to "get in," but he didn't want to let go of his hatred and bias against undesirable, unlovely, and unworthy neighbours. Suppose he could be in charge of determining precisely who his neighbour was. In that case, he could select only loveable people as neighbours and quietly sneak into the kingdom of God with his hate still in tact.

Jesus was not fooled. He responded by sharing the parable of The Good Samaritan, which blows up any possibility of hatred sneaking into God's kingdom.

Looking for a loophole just like me, the religious leader asked, "And just how would you define 'neighbour'?"

> Jesus replied with a story. "A Jewish man was travelling from Jerusalem down to Jericho, and he was attacked by bandits. They stripped him of his clothes, beat him up, and left him half dead beside the road. By chance a priest came along. But when he saw the man lying there, he crossed to the other side of the road and passed him by. A Temple assistant walked over and looked at him lying there, but he also passed by on the other side. Then a despised Samaritan came along, and when he saw the man, he felt compassion for him. Going over to him, the Samaritan soothed his wounds with olive oil and wine and bandaged them. Then he put the man on his own

donkey and took him to an inn, where he took care of him. The next day he handed the innkeeper two silver coins, telling him, 'Take care of this man. If his bill runs higher than this, I'll pay you the next time I'm here.'

"Now which of these three would you say was a neighbour to the man who was attacked by bandits?" Jesus asked.

The man replied, "The one who showed him mercy."

Then Jesus said, "Yes, now go and do the same."

The point still lands 2000 years later. The injured man was Jewish. The priest and the Levite were Jews; they were supposed to take care of their own, but they didn't because of fear and preoccupation with self-righteousness. The Samaritan was the arch-enemy of the Jew. Jews and Samaritans had been successfully killing each other for 600 years. When Jesus said, "A Samaritan travelling the road came on him," the religious leader would have immediately thought, "Oh no, that's terrible! Of all the people to come down the road, why does it have to be a Samaritan? That scumbag will probably go up to the injured Jew and finish him off. I know the truth about those despicable people! This is exactly why I can't be a neighbour to them."

Of course, Jesus turned the story on its head, and the religious leader snapped out of his racist, hate-filled thoughts. The Samaritan loved the person he was supposed to hate.

This story travelled through time and landed right in the middle of the mess with my dad. No, I did not like him. In so many ways, my dad and I were just like the Jew and the Samaritan from

Jesus' culture-smashing story. My dad was my neighbour, and my dad was also hurting badly. Could I just carelessly pass him by?

Jesus' story from so long ago rewrote the narrative of hate I had so carefully scripted for my life. Jesus opened my eyes to see what was better. At the same time, I felt that actually loving my dad was an unreachable peak, and I still had plenty of doubts. How could it be good for me to love and honour my father, as the Scriptures say? Wouldn't I just be opening myself up to abuse? Isn't respecting the unworthy a bad idea?

I had to make a choice. Would I trust the ancient stories of Jesus and begin looking for ways to honour my father, or would I continue on the path of hatred, resentment, bitterness, and revenge?

After two weeks of intense conversations, I repented of my hatred and disrespect towards my father. I was making the most significant, countercultural, counterintuitive decision of my life. My instinct was to retaliate when hit, and now I was going to come home and take all his garbage and return it with a blessing? All because some grand, overarching story told me to? I must admit, I wasn't convinced it was the right call. I asked Marty for some help. "What do I do?" I asked him. "I don't feel any love for him. I'm going to go home and apologize, but then what?"

Marty smiled as he pulled a list of 40 ways in which I could honour my father out of his pocket. I thanked him, took the list, and jumped on the bus for the long ride home. When I got home, I apologized and then started dutifully going through the list. At first, I didn't feel like it, but over time something incredible happened. My heart of hatred sprang a leak, all that dark stuff began to drain out, and a spirit of love replaced it. The way of redeeming love had captured me. It was the better story!

Over 30 years have come and gone since that transformative summer. Sadly, my dad has never changed in all that time. He is still the same disappointing dad. But I changed. Divine love replaced my own story of bitterness, resentment, and justified rage. That has made all the difference in my life. With my dad, sometimes the best way I could honour him was to leave him alone. Loving and respecting someone doesn't mean you allow yourself to be abused by them. We all have to experience the consequences of the poor choices we make in life, and my dad is no exception. Sadly, his choices make a close friendship with him impossible for me, but because of divine love's healing presence in my life, I can still honour, respect, and forgive my dad instead of hating him. The Jesus story I chose to shape my life around all those years ago as a teenager changed my life forever for the better.

Interestingly, all this happened without my feelings being exactly in the right place. My desires were mixed. My short-term desires were to poke my dad in the eye and flip him the bird. The Jesus way helped me long for better things that reside beyond my immediate emotions and circumstances. Often, we are blinded by the sudden, reactionary emotions that bubble up when we endure difficult situations. Unseen trauma in our own story can produce volcanic reactions that feel right in the moment but make us miserable long term. This is why the habitual embrace of an overarching story that has love, grace, forgiveness, and hope at its centre is so important. Life is too hard to live without it.

Part Three
Yeah, but what about...

> *Whenever we read the obscene stories, the voluptuous debaucheries, the cruel and torturous executions, the unrelenting vindictiveness with which more than half the Bible is filled, it would be more consistent that we call it the word of a demon than the word of God. It is a history of wickedness that has served to corrupt and brutalize humankind.*
> Thomas Paine

During our food and philosophy nights, in addition to many other discussions around town with non-Christian friends, one objection to Christianity came up over and over again: the bad stuff in the Bible. The Bible promotes slavery, crushes women, and seems like a big fan of genocide. Isn't the hell of the Bible antithetical to the good news? And what are we to make of those retrograde views on sex? These "problem passages" created insurmountable barriers to belief for the people I was interacting with, as they often did for me. Early in my Christian experience, my Bible reading time was very valuable. It helped centre me for the day, and I benefited greatly from the wisdom it offered. However, as the years went by, I found myself coming up against cringe-worthy passages. "This is messed up," I would mutter to myself, and then quickly glance skyward, hoping lightning bolts from the heavens wouldn't strike me down for my blasphemy! Is a genuine belief in the Christian story still possible in the face of these passages that burn so badly in the ear of our modern sensibilities?

In this final section of the book, I will lay out some food for thought that has helped me see these difficult Scriptures in a more balanced light. These observations are not air-tight arguments designed to answer all questions and squelch all doubts. However, they have offered some help as I contemplate difficult passages.

Before we dive in, I wish to call attention to one observation from the brilliant mind of historian and celebrated author Tom Holland.

Tom Holland walked away from the Christian story as a youth, labelling it as false and weak. As an adult, he threw himself passionately into studying pre-Christian cultures. As he buried himself in long hours of research on Rome, Greece, and Persia, he experienced a stunning realization: he was horrified by the brutality and callousness of these ancient peoples. Then the shoe dropped for him: the bad taste in his mouth for the ancient world had come because his sensibilities had remained fundamentally Christian. Those Christian sensibilities he assumed to be weak were just the opposite. The strength of Christian virtue had made a better world: human rights, the intrinsic value of each person, equality, the virtue of sacrificial love, the vital importance of free inquiry, care for the poor and sick, freedom of conscience, and our fundamental understanding of good and evil, to name just a few, all flow from the headwaters of the Christian story. They do not come from the ancient pre-Christian era or somehow magically appear during the "Enlightenment" period. They stem from imperfect people trying as best they could to shape their lives around the story of Jesus.

Holland had stumbled upon a great irony: those who flatly reject the Christian religion do so based on Christian principles!

For example, Charles Darwin rejected Christianity for materialistic evolution, not because science precluded the possibility of God, but because there was such misery in the world. Holland writes:

One [objection to God] more than any other haunted [Darwin]:

a species of parasitic wasp. "I cannot persuade myself that a beneficent and omnipotent God would have designed and created the Ichneumonidæ with the express intention of their feeding within the living bodies of caterpillars."[61]

The general ethos of the ancient world would not have had such a moral objection to this observation of cruelty. Darwin turned away from God precisely because his sensibilities were fundamentally Christian.

Whenever I feel uncomfortable with something I'm reading in my Bible, it is helpful to realize that the discomfort is based on Christian sensibilities instilled into me and our Western culture through the generations. This realization doesn't solve troubling Biblical issues, but it does set them in proper perspective. Without Christianity, no one would even care about the problem passages. They wouldn't matter. With this in the front of my mind, I turn now towards the problems.

End Notes:

[61] Holland, *Dominion*, 439.

Chapter 17

Do life's brutality and the absence of God ruin the better story?

Is Christianity just one good story among many that ultimately get corrupted, as my Palestinian friend says? Maybe Natasha is correct in her belief that imaginary powers should not be credited for the strength she needed to survive a brutal world. What about Ishmael, who warns that the most dangerous cage in the world is not the mortal one; but rather the religious one? And what of Jacob and AJ, two very religious people who employ God as a bludgeoning stick upon their enemies—doesn't that sufficiently ruin any better story that connects itself to God?

For many, life is just too dark to believe in redemptive love. I've felt it in my friends—and in myself. Life's tangled mess does make it harder to look beyond the struggle to a hope that transcends our here and now.

Mistin and I were on a short-term mission trip to Mozambique. We taught Bible lessons and ran a kids club; we even had a nurse's station to help the sick. We did some good. One little boy with a thorn embedded in his foot could not walk because of the infection. Our team gave him minor surgery and cleaned out the wound, making a massive difference in the boy's life. Before we left, his crutches were gone, and he was playing soccer again with his friends. We were encouraged; we even praised the Lord. God had done good work on that boy's foot, we told ourselves.

One day a woman showed up in a wheelbarrow. Her husband had pushed her for two days through the jungle. Somehow, they had heard we were coming. The man pleaded with us to do something. Our nurse perceived that the woman probably had AIDS and didn't have long to live. We gave the woman a Tylenol, and we set about praying that God would heal her body. If ever there was a time for God to manifest his power, this was it! We were even in Africa. The West is chronically underrepresented by miraculous happenings, but not Africa! We beseeched the Almighty with all the faith and fervour we could muster.

The woman died. Her emaciated corpse slumped unceremoniously in the bottom of the wheelbarrow like a sack of rotten potatoes. With a vacant look, the heartbroken man carted his dear wife back into the jungle. In that moment of desperate need, God appeared to be absent. The hero of our story had disappeared. So much for all the many Bible verses that promise healing and deliverance. In the realm of my lived experience, it is in these moments that the pull back into the mortal cage is the strongest. I want to sense God's presence in my own life and see it in the lives of my friends, but more times than I care to admit, I simply don't see, hear, or feel much of anything beyond the mortal cage. The Bible verses making big promises that never come true mock me in my despair.

The story tells me that I am a vital part of the hero's presence

As Kate Bowler continued to suffer through her stage-four cancer, she made the following observation:

> At a time when I should have felt abandoned by God, I was not reduced to ashes. I felt like I was floating, floating on the love and prayers of all those who hummed around me like worker bees, bringing notes and flowers and warm socks and quilts embroidered with words of encouragement. They came in like priests and mirrored back to me the face of Jesus....I did not tell them how few of their words are needed but how much their hands are wanted, a hand on my back as I tear up, a hand on my head for a soft prayer for healing. When I feel I am fading away, these hands prop me up and make me new.... Joy persists somehow, and I soak in it. Life is so beautiful, life is so hard.[62]

The best thing I can do as a member of the fraternity of uneasy believers is sit in the dust with the grieving, curse with the devastated, cry with the brokenhearted, and shake my head in sorrow with the downcast. We don't have answers about God's seeming lack of involvement, only the hope that in the suffering, others might glimpse transcendent love and experience some measure of comfort from our compassionate presence in their suffering.

Ours is the only story with a suffering saviour

At the blazing centre of the better story, we find a suffering saviour: Jesus, abandoned by God, alone on the cross, bleeding out in pain and agony. When thoughts of a greater purpose vanish and chaos reigns. When everything falls apart and the way forward is dark. When prayers are not answered and God seems absent. When the mortal cage tightens itself around me like a boa constrictor, I can hear Jesus cry out with my same frustration, "My God, my God, why have you forsaken me?" Jesus experienced the same abandonment I feel. Jesus has all the same scars I do. There is some consolation in that.

Life is hard no matter what you believe

Every human alive today shapes their life around a story built on faith. Does life bound inside a mortal cage with random chance as its founding principle make life any easier or offer greater consolation amid our suffering? Not that I can see. There are many shaping stories we humans cling to—Islam, Buddhism, Hinduism, secularism, humanism—the list goes on. None of them dissipate life's difficulties, so we have to ask which of the stories offers a better path through the suffering and silence we all must endure. To me, the answer is obvious.

End Notes:

[62] Bowler, *Everything Happens for a Reason and Other Lies I've Loved*, 121.

Chapter 18

Does the Bible's support of slavery ruin the better story?

The Bible supports the institution of slavery, and that's a problem. Here are some examples:

- "You who are slaves must submit to your masters with all respect. Do what they tell you—not only if they are kind and reasonable, but even if they are cruel." (1 Peter 2:18)

- "All slaves should show full respect for their masters so they will not bring shame on the name of God and his teaching." (1 Timothy 6:1)

- "Slaves, obey your earthly masters in everything you do. Try to please them all the time, not just when they are watching you. Serve them sincerely because of your reverent fear of the

Lord." (Colossians 3:22)

- "If you buy a Hebrew slave, he may serve no more than six years. Set him free in the seventh year, and he will owe you nothing for his freedom...When a man sells his daughter as a slave, she will not be freed at the end of six years as the men are." (Exodus 21:2, 7)

- "Slaves must always obey their masters and do their best to please them. They must not talk back." (Titus 2:9)

- "If anyone beats his male or female slave with a club and the slave dies as a result, the owner must be punished. But if the slave recovers within a day or two, then the owner shall not be punished, since the slave is his property." (Exodus 21:20-21)

- "However, you may purchase male and female slaves from among the nations around you. You may also purchase the children of temporary residents who live among you, including those who have been born in your land. You may treat them as your property, passing them on to your children as a permanent inheritance. You may treat them as slaves, but you must never treat your fellow Israelites this way." (Leviticus 25:44-46)

Let's take stock of what we just read. An enslaved person under both the Old and New Testament guidelines was considered the property of another. The enslaved were expected to obey their masters in all things. Masters could abuse their slaves under the Old Testament law to the very point of death. The only line that was not to be crossed when disciplining enslaved people was killing them; that was a divine no-no, but if it did happen, the master was given a relative slap on the wrist for his indiscrete moment of passion. The New Testament has a lot more to say about the importance of treating slaves with respect than the Old Testament does, but the slave was still considered property.

If the grand story of God is so good, why is the institution of slavery so wholly baked into it? Why wouldn't Yahweh, along with circumcision and Sabbath-keeping, throw in freedom as one of the distinctive marks of his chosen people? Why would Jesus remain silent on the issue? Why in the New Testament do we find only the seeds of the abolition movement but not the full flower? Christian history reveals that for centuries these seeds of abolition, which many of us recognize today, were not enough to convince Christian slave owners that owning another human was wrong.

The very idea of slavery is repulsive to our modern notions of freedom and morality, especially after the dehumanization of enslaved Africans during the founding years of North and South America. How can the Bible be good if its very words seem to give colonial slaveholders a free pass? We can't just ignore these verses, especially since many have used them to brutalize countless humans.

When I approach this thorny issue, I first try to consider the overall message of the Bible, and ask how that message shaped the direction of history. Does the grand, overarching story of redemption push people away from the institution of slavery or towards it? The historical record gives a clear answer to this critical question. The message of freedom and equality in Christ, which results in mutual service and love for all people, sets humanity on a trajectory away from slavery. The Apostle Paul encapsulates the Bible's grand vision for humanity well when he dramatically unifies the message of both testaments: "For you have been called to live in freedom, my brothers and sisters. But don't use your freedom to satisfy your sinful nature. Instead, use your freedom to serve one another in love. For the whole law can be summed up in this one command: 'Love your neighbour as yourself." (Galatians 5:13-14)

The overwhelming consensus of nearly every people group and religion in the ancient world was that slavery was a perfectly acceptable institution. Only Christianity pushed back against this stratified version of the human order. Freedom's message acted like a beaver chewing away at the base of a thick tree. It would take awhile, but the tree would eventually fall.

As early as the fourth century, Augustine, the Bishop of Hippo, was preaching against slavery. He used the church's funds regularly to purchase the freedom of enslaved people. He referred to these church-funded freedom events as "acts of piety." Augustine was convinced that slavery was not close to God's heart, and those that embraced the way of Jesus must reject it. His words and actions moved his congregation to such a degree that they boarded a slave ship and, on the threat of violence, demanded that the slaves be freed.[63]

In the seventh century, we meet Bathilde, a slave girl harvested from the shores of England and pressed into slavery in the Frankish dominions. Fortune smiled on this hard-working girl far from home when Clovis II, King of the Franks, noticed her and, defying the social convention of the day, married her! When Clovis died an untimely death, Bathilde became regent until her sons were old enough to rule. She used her position of authority and influence to fight against slavery.

Bathilde lowered taxes on peasants so they would stop selling their children. She proceeded to buy and free slaves with money from her own treasury, and with the help of the Frankish church, she outlawed the purchase and sale of any new slaves. Slavery still existed in her realms among some nobility, but she had struck a mighty blow against it. Bathilde's abolitionist work was utterly unique in the world of her day. While she waged her personal religious war against slavery, the institution continued unabated everywhere else in the world. Thanks to her, this was no longer true in Western Europe. Her influence cannot be overstated—when the Franks invaded Great Britain in 1066 under the Duke of Normandy, they immediately outlawed slavery upon conquest (more than 20% of England was enslaved). It wasn't long after this that holding enslaved people anywhere in Western Europe was abolished. Enslaved people coming to European territory were freed. Bathilde acted according to her deeply held religious convictions. She had no other reason to abolish slavery than that it didn't fit with the Jesus story around which she shaped her life.[64]

When African slavery to the Western realms reared its ugly head in the 16th century, the Roman Catholic Church consistently and forcefully rejected the idea. One papal bull after another came down from Rome condemning slavery in the strongest possible terms: excommunication.[65] You could not be a good Catholic and own slaves. Unfortunately, the influence of the Roman church was in decline during this time; nation states were flexing their muscles, and religion was not welcome to interfere. Spain and Portugal were Catholic nations, but they disobeyed the official Catholic position. Spain objected to church dogma on this issue to such a degree that they sacked Rome in 1527. The African slave trade did not come about as a Christian religious rite; rather, it flourished because nationalism had been steadily pushing aside

Christian influence. The nationalistic designs to be wealthy and powerful led to slave atrocities (among other things) far more than any flimsy biblical justifications did. Jesuit missionaries were forbidden by their nationalistic overlords to read the Papal Bulls condemning slavery in the New World. When they did anyway, they were labelled traitors and killed. Still, Catholic missionaries persisted in the New World with anti-slavery perspectives. The Catholics of the French and Spanish colonies were the first to write law codes that helped to better the lives of enslaved people and put them on a path to freedom.[66]

The Protestants were indeed late to the game in comparison with the Catholics. They clutched their pro-slavery Bible verses a bit too tightly, but once they managed to push aside their nationalist interests and get back to the gospel message of love and freedom, they realized their proof texts could not hold up. The tea, molasses, tobacco, cotton, and sugar were lovely, but once the veil of ignorance was lifted and Christians began to realize the brutal cost of these luxuries, the days of slavery were once again numbered. In the end, the Christians of the British Empire were responsible for bringing down an institution nearly as old as humankind! If it wasn't for the liberating story of Jesus, could this global shift away from slavery have happened? Outspoken Christian statesman William Wilberforce and numerous other followers of Jesus worked tirelessly to end the dehumanizing African slave trade in the British Empire precisely because of their faith.

This same liberating faith motivated thousands of white American Christians to campaign against the South before the American Civil War and fill the Union ranks during the war. Naturally, the Civil War was more complicated than just the slavery issue, but abolition was the central theme of this great conflagration.[67]

The grand story of God, illustrated by Moses marching an enslaved nation out of Egypt, and Jesus' proclamations that those who wish to be free are free indeed, gave many Black Americans enough incentive to keep the faith of the slaveholder after they obtained their freedom. Even the enslaved knew what the better story taught about their situation. Any version of Christianity tuned into the overarching story of Jesus has never been nor will ever support dehumanization. A similar situation is happening today, as predominantly Christian people work courageously to end modern-day slavery as found in the global human sex-trafficking crisis.

A clear picture emerges when I take the long view of history: Christianity consistently and tirelessly opposes slavery, that great enemy of human flourishing.

End Notes:

[63] See http://www.augnet.org/en/works-of-augustine/his-impact/2437-slavery/

[64] See https://patriceayme.wordpress.com/2015/05/10/a-truth-france-outlawed-slavery-1355-years-ago/https://www.biola.edu/blogs/good-book-blog/2015/from-slave-to-queen-to-nun-advancing-the-kingdom-of-god-through-vocation

[65] Robert Goodwin, *Spain the Centre of the World* 1519-1682 (New York: Bloomsbury, 2016), 99.

[66] The ideas behind this paragraph are supported by numerous examples from Rodney Stark's, *Bearing False Witness*, David Hart's *Atheist Delusions* and Robert Goodwin's *Spain the Centre of the World*.

[67] For dozens and dozens of pages of primary source material supporting the claim that slavery was the primary cause of the American Civil war, read Ron Chernow's *Grant* (New York: Penguin Press, 2017).

Chapter 19

Do the Bible's sexist perspectives ruin the better story?

The Bible seems to muzzle women and shove them in a corner. If that's true, it's a problem! Here are some examples:

- "Women should be silent during the church meetings. It is not proper for them to speak. They should be submissive, just as the law says. If they have any questions, they should ask their husbands at home, for it is improper for women to speak in church meetings." (1 Corinthians 14:34-35)

- "Women should learn quietly and submissively. I do not let women teach men or have authority over them. Let them listen quietly. For God made Adam first, and afterward he made Eve. And it was not Adam who was deceived by Satan. The woman was deceived, and sin was the result. But women will be saved through childbearing, assuming they continue to live in faith, love, holiness, and modesty." (1 Timothy 2:11-15)

- "For wives, this means submit to your husbands as to the Lord. For a husband is the head of his wife as Christ is the head of the church. He is the Saviour of his body, the church. As the church submits to Christ, so you wives should submit to your husbands in everything." (Ephesians 5:22-24)

For many liberated women of today, these commands are just too repressive. Is it finally time to bury Christianity in a shallow grave, seeing it for the retrograde, antiquated albatross that it is?

However, thankfully, these three passages of Scripture that appear uncharitable to women are not the entire story.

Women were drawn to Jesus' message precisely because he broke down long-established walls of patriarchal superiority. Jesus' faithful demolition of the status quo is what made him a scandal. He mortified the earthly powers not just through his teaching but by his example. This otherworldly rabbi regularly did the unthinkable by hanging out with women and children, sick people, prostitutes, and Samaritans. Anyone marginalized by gender or status was welcomed in, loved, empowered, and liberated. The abundant New Testament record of female involvement in Christian ministry at all levels is undoubtedly the most radical, culture-breaking celebration of empowered women in human history.

- A woman led a worship service memorializing the death of Jesus. She did it without permission and regardless of what the men thought. Jesus was blessed by it (John 12:1-4).

- Mark goes out of his way to include women in his expanded list of disciples. (Mark 15:40-41)

- Jesus commissions women to be the first evangelists of his resurrection. (Matthew 28:10, John 20:17)

- The ancient prophecy of Joel 2:28-29 was fulfilled when the spirit of God was given equally to men and women at Pentecost. (Acts 1:17)

- Luke makes a point to let us know that women were a significant part of the early Church. (Acts 5:14, 8:12, 17:4)

- The first church in Europe was begun, organized, and sustained by women—Lydia, in particular (Acts 16). It is also remarkable that the disciples "sat down to speak with the women" (v13), as that was certainly not the cultural norm.

- Paul's thank-you list at the end of Romans is a "who's who" for the early Church. Almost a third of the people named are women (Romans 16:3-12).

- One early church was co-led by a husband-wife team, Priscilla and Aquila. Both Luke and Paul put Priscilla's name first. Having the woman's name in the priority position would have been entirely inappropriate for first-century culture unless a new and better story was changing cultural norms. (Acts 18:26, Romans 16, 1 Corinthians 16:19)

- Phoebe was a leader in the church, and Paul bestows authority on her by ordering both men and women to do whatever she asks of them. (Romans 16:1-2)

- Junia is a woman who is "outstanding among the apostles" (Romans 16:7). Some scholars have made great efforts to recast her as a man, but for the first 300 or more years of Christian history, this was not the case. In particular, John Chrysostom (349 AD) says of the passage where we find Junia: "To be an apostle is something great. But to be outstanding among the apostles, just think what a wonderful song of praise that is. Indeed, what wonderful wisdom this woman must have had to be deemed great among the apostles."[68]

- Paul gives instructions to both men and women praying and prophesying together in public worship. (1 Corinthians 11:4-5)

- Jesus let Mary "sit at his feet" (Luke 10:39). This phrase is not a throw-away line; it indicates a student-teacher relationship. It meant that Mary was being taught by Jesus so that one day Mary could teach, just like Paul "sat at the feet" of Gamaliel. Rabbi Jesus' education of Mary was utterly scandalous and probably one of the primary reasons Martha was so agitated. It was not Mary's place as a woman to be a rabbi-in-training. But Jesus did not have a problem with it.[69]

For the first time in human memory, a worldview had come to the fore, powerfully resisting the functional class system between the genders. According to Jesus, women were not inferior. This was big news in the first century! The message was clear: there is true equality when joining God's family in Christ. No other faith story blessed, encouraged, and empowered women like the Christian one. This radical equality caused Paul to throw down the gauntlet with his now-famous cry for equality in Galatians 3:28: "There is no longer Jew or Gentile, slave or free, male and female. For you are all one in Christ Jesus." The unity and freedom of Jesus' message cracked the very foundations of the established order.

But before we get too excited about all this culture-smashing radical equality, we have to acknowledge that the early Church pumped the brakes hard on the whole egalitarianism thing. We can easily see nearly two thousand years of female subjugation that continues today. Many modern Christians still largely ignore the biblical examples of liberated women and instead choose to take the three Pauline imperatives as their marching orders for establishing policies regarding women. Of course, they would not use the term subjugation; that sounds cruel. In today's parlance, the term is "complementary." This means women and men have distinct, inflexible roles in church and family life; the genders complement each other best when men rule and lead and women help and support. For much of my life, I also believed that true human flourishing is only possible when both women and men understand their roles and live obediently in them.

Adding to the complementarian argument is the observation that the Scriptures consistently have men in leadership, whether as priests, kings, or patriarchs of households. In contrast, women are limited to supportive roles. We see the patriarchal tenor of Scripture in the Apostle Paul's list of requirements for elders that he assumes will be male. "The elder must be the husband of one wife," he instructs Timothy and Titus, not the other way around.

We find ourselves in a conundrum. On the one hand, numerous Biblical examples celebrate women who are free to live out their giftings, whatever they may be. On the other hand, a few passages agree with the accepted patriarchal flow of history throughout the biblical era. So which is it? For the most part, the church joined its culture and elevated these patriarchal passages to shape their perspectives on women. The result over the last two millennia has been the muzzling of many talented and gifted women.

Finally, however, times might be changing. Scholarship is adding increased nuance to these crucial passages that have been used to keep women in their place. For example, eminent teacher and theologian John Stackhouse has mused about how obscure one of those troubling passages really is:

> I had been reading yet another explanation of 1 Timothy 2:11-15, easily one of the most obscure of the classic passages on this matter. I remember quite clearly now, more than 20 years later, putting the book down on my lap and realizing this insight: nobody could explain this passage. To be sure, I had been reading more than a dozen attempts to explain this passage. Some of them were ingenious. A few were even likely, but it struck me with paradigm-shaking force that no one could explain all the clauses in this passage with full plausibility. I then began to think that this problem was true, not only of expositions of this one text, but of the whole gender question. No one I had read, and I had read quite a few, could put all the relevant texts together into a single finished puzzle with no pieces left over — with none manufactured to fill in gaps and with none forced into place.[70]

Stackhouse taps out on the question altogether! In his view, no one can know what 1 Timothy 2:11-15 is talking about. David Bentley Hart piles into the discussion by tossing out whole verses altogether. He aims his guns at 1 Corinthians 14:34-35, where Paul says, "Women should be silent during church meetings":

These verses are a considerable textual problem, as they clearly constitute an interpolation that breaks the flow of the text, and that seems written in a voice unlike Paul's, and that contradicts other passages in Paul. Simply on its face, the argument reads coherently only when the verses are removed.

He then launches into a reasonably thorough investigation of the creative ways in which many of the ancient manuscripts interrupt, displace, footnote, or otherwise disturb the placement of these two verses. Hart concludes his observations with the following comments: "In any event, the best critical scholarship regards these verses as later and rather maladroit interpolations... the evidence preponderantly indicates that they are almost certainly spurious."[71]

Hart is arguing that these verses don't even belong in the Bible. If that's true, we owe an apology to women for messing them up for about 1,800 years of church history! Whether they belong or not, it is clear that the influence these few verses have had on women's lives in church history has been far stronger than necessary.

I'm not sure the Church has ever felt quite right about its stance that limits the potential of women. I know I felt that way, but I was—so I thought—being obedient to God's instructions on the matter. Reflecting with me about this, my wife shares her frustration of being excluded from the leadership meetings when we started our church plant. She is a strong leader like me and had great ideas, but to have her in the room of leaders was out of the question. I didn't like this, so I found other ways to maximize her abilities. Churches the world over do this. We find creative ways to help women use their leadership gifts while still technically not "disobeying" the Pauline imperatives. For example, many churches let women lead and speak so long as they are technically under the authority of a man. Other churches let women lead and speak by withholding an official leadership title. Still others let women lead and teach children, teens, and other women, just not men. Others justify women teaching by changing the nomenclature of what they are doing—instead of preaching, they are "sharing," "giving testimony," or "leading worship." Historically, Christian women have found additional clever loopholes to escape the strangling effects of the Timothy and Corinthian passages. For example, if a woman became a single foreign missionary, she was allowed more far-reaching leadership privileges.

Looking into all the ways women have served in church settings, regardless of how seriously their environments took these passages, I realized one thing: no church applies these passages in any strictly literal sense. Women are not silent in church. They do influence men, and nobody insists that a woman's salvation comes literally through their childbearing.

The seeds of women's liberation were planted by Jesus; no other story has done that. Granted, these have taken longer to germinate than we impatient and chronologically snobbish moderns would have liked. Additionally, the way some Christians in particular have stood in the way of equality during our more modern suffrage and women's liberation movements has been hard to watch. But the seeds are there—they come from nowhere else.

Far too many women are still held back from reaching their full potential by virtue of their gender. But I believe the seeds of liberation stemming from the Christian story offer the best hope for women in cultures around the world, too many of which still see women as inferior. I was reminded of this sad reality when reading the award-winning book *I am Malala*. In it, Malala Yousafzai shares that the ultimate put-down for a Pashtun man is to say; "He actually listens to his wife." Malala stood up for women's equality, though sadly, she took a bullet to the head for her bravery. What was her crime that caused a man to try to blow her brains out? She wanted to get an education like the boys in her country. Equality isn't baked into the Muslim system, so there is a long road ahead for courageous women like Malala who are connected to that religion. Perhaps they will find their way. I hope so. Overarching stories do shape the direction of our lives; the Christian story, more than any other, carries with it the fertile seeds of equality, which will inevitably grow despite all efforts to prevent it, even by well-meaning Christians loyal to Pauline imperatives.

End Notes:

[68] Hart, *The New Testament*, 317.

[69] Unpublished notes from Darrell Johnson, formerly lead pastor of First Baptist Church Vancouver B.C.

[70] Sarah Bessy, *Jesus Feminist* (Newark, NJ: Audible, 2013) Chapter 6 1:39:10.

[71] Hart, *The New Testament*, 346.

Chapter 20

Does the Bible's support of genocide ruin the better story?

It was his 32nd birthday party. I'm not much of a night owl, but my friend insisted that I join him at the pub to celebrate the passing of another year. The birthday boy had an eclectic group of friends. When they weren't excusing themselves to smoke weed out front or hammering down another pilsner, I got a chance to get to know a few of them. One tipsy gal seemed especially friendly; as we chatted, I learned she was a Ph.D. candidate at UBC who had gone to high school with my friend. The invitation to his birthday party seemed like a good time for her to get reacquainted and have a night out away from all her responsibilities at the university. We enjoyed lots of laughter and spirited conversation, but her happy demeanour changed when she found out what I did for a living. She put her hand on her head and groaned when I told her I was a minister.

"I'm an atheist!" She proclaimed, slamming her near-empty beer glass down on the table.

Trying to keep things light, I shrugged my shoulders and gave her a quizzical look. "Why on earth would you ever want to be an atheist?" I asked with a smile.

The answer was immediate, though slurred by intemperance: "The geonnishide pashegesh!"

Even in her inebriated state, the genocide passages still sparked her volcanic rejection of Christianity. She was in no mood (or condition!) for discussion. I gave her my card and asked if she might like to come to church sometime or discuss the matter further in more sober moments. She told me in no uncertain terms that she would never come to church, nor would she be interested in continuing the conversation—now or ever. "How about those Canucks?" I offered, attempting to change the subject.

Richard Dawkins, "atheism's most prolific televangelist," as one author referred to him, lambasts the God of the Old Testament as a jealous, proud, petty, unjust, unforgiving, vindictive, bloodthirsty...(he goes on and on) malevolent bully![72] Genocide fits well within the *modus operandi* of a God such as this. For Dawkins and my tipsy friend, the possibility of believing a better story is beyond remote if it comes from the same pages of the book where God mandates the wholesale slaughter of entire people groups.

It's not that they don't have a point. Here are a few disheartening examples:

- In the Old Testament, Samuel the Prophet says to Saul, the first king of the Israelites, "It was the Lord who told me to anoint you as king of his people, Israel. Now listen to this message from the Lord! This is what the Lord of Heaven's Armies has declared: I have decided to settle accounts with the nation of Amalek for opposing Israel when they came from Egypt. Now go and completely destroy the entire Amalekite nation—men, women, children, babies, cattle, sheep, goats, camels, and donkeys." (1 Samuel 15:1-3)

- "The people of Samaria must bear the consequences of their guilt because they rebelled against their God. They will be killed by an invading army, their little ones dashed to death against the ground, their pregnant women ripped open by swords." (Hosea 13:16)

- Then the Lord said to me, "Look, I have begun to hand King Sihon and his land over to you. Begin now to conquer and occupy his land.' Then King Sihon declared war on us and mobilized his forces at Jahaz. But the Lord our God handed him over to us, and we crushed him, his sons, and all his people. We conquered all his towns and completely destroyed everyone—men, women, and children. Not a single person was spared. We took all the livestock as plunder for ourselves, along with anything of value from the towns we ransacked." (Deuteronomy 2:31-35)

- So Moses said to the people, "Choose some men, and arm them to fight the Lord's war of revenge against Midian."... They attacked Midian as the Lord had commanded Moses, and they killed all the men....Then the Israelite army captured the Midianite women and children and seized their cattle and flocks and all their wealth as plunder. They burned all the towns and villages where the Midianites had lived. After they had gathered the plunder and captives, both people and animals, they brought them all to Moses and Eleazar the priest, and to the whole community of Israel... But Moses was furious with all the generals and captains who had returned from the battle. "Why have you let all the women live?" he demanded. "These are the very ones who followed Balaam's advice and caused the people of Israel to rebel against the Lord at Mount Peor. They are the ones who caused the plague to strike the Lord's people. So kill all the boys and all the women who have had intercourse with a man. Only the young girls who are virgins may live; you may keep them for yourselves." (Numbers 31:1-20)

Is there an explanation? Not one that eliminates the violent transition of the Jewish people from slavery, to wandering Bedouins, to a settled people, to a conquering nation. The world is a violent place, and divine intervention of any kind has never really prevented human carnage. But is there anything that can take the hard edge off all the heaven-sanctioned bludgeoning we find in the Bible?

First, rhetorical exaggeration was in vogue. Written accounts were full of bravado and "trash talk," which didn't reflect reality. To be sure, many died, but not nearly as many as was indicated. In Joshua 10, for example, the author boasts six times that Israel did not leave a single survivor in one battle or another. Yet throughout the book of Joshua and Judges, we regularly discover that there are survivors all over the place. They are not helpless refugees either; the forces arrayed against Israel are strong and dug in. At the conclusion of Joshua's struggle to take over the promised land, we discover another rhetorical flourish that is optimistic beyond credulity. Joshua 21:43-45 says:

And Yahweh gave to Israel all the land that he swore to give to their ancestors, and they took possession of it and settled in it. Yahweh gave them rest on every side, according to all that he had sworn to their ancestors, and nobody from all their enemies withstood them, for Yahweh had given all their enemies into their hand. And nothing failed from all the good things that Yahweh promised to the house of Israel; everything came to pass.

This is simply post-war propaganda. Joshua 13 contradicts the optimistic summary of Joshua 21. Judges 12 goes into a point-by-point list of Israel's failures: Manasseh did not drive out Beth-Sean, and its towns, or Taanach and its towns, or the inhabitants of Dor and its villages, or the inhabitants of Ibleam and its towns, or the inhabitants of Megiddo and its towns; the Canaanites were determined to live in this land; Ephraim did not drive out the Canaanites living in Gezer, so the Canaanites lived in their midst in Gezer...and on and on it goes. The scattered celebrations found in both books are no different than when I brag about "destroying all opposition" when playing hockey, or taking down my son and "crushing him like a little grape" in a wrestling match. They are "power words" meant to encourage one side of a struggle. Every Jew who read these words of wartime encouragement knew they weren't true in any literal sense. Hence, the authors had no trouble writing in chest-bumping, high-fiving passages right alongside their rather depressing accounts of military mediocrity.

Second, what Scripture records was not an account of genocide; the record is one of protracted tribal warfare in which there were no clear winners. All the groups involved had a claim on the land. The Jewish claim dated back 500 years; the other tribes had claims of their own. War happened, as it does. And yes, the Israelites managed by some miracle as a rag-tag bunch of desert wanderers to overcome incredible odds and conquer 31 kings in their campaign. People died, as is the case with war. But at best, it was a toe-hold in the land. Beyond those killed, hundreds of other kings and tribal leaders scattered about the promised land survived. As history marched forward, these people groups continued to fight for what they thought belonged to them, but they also managed to make peace and intermarry, to split up again and then fight some more, as happens on almost every piece of contested real estate on the earth.

Third, it's helpful to see the redemptive arc throughout the entire story of God. War happens, but God still works through it or even despite it. From the Christian point of view, the violent events surrounding the nation of Israel's beginning are part of a grand story that ultimately unites all humanity under the banner of divine love. Canaanites and Moabites were both tribes under God's condemnation. Still, it's no accident that a Canaanite woman from the city of Jericho survives the invasion of Israel to become the ancestor of King David. He would go on to become the ancestor of Jesus Christ. It's not a fluke that a Moabite woman named Ruth also finds herself in the Messianic ancestral line. The Messiah has both Canaanite and Moabite blood in his veins! Few, if any nations have managed to avoid bloodshed in their coming of age. Israel is no exception. As recorded in the Bible, Israel's history is not fundamentally about the superiority of a race and its justification to slaughter its opponents. Instead, the record is there so all humanity might glimpse the redemptive thread that precariously but undeniably marches forward throughout history towards the person of Jesus and the salvation of all humankind.

Finally, for those offended by an ancient tribe that managed to use God as a primary motivating factor to displace other tribes and secure a home for themselves, I ask, why care at all? It makes sense for me to have a moral dilemma, as one who believes in an overarching story of divine love. It's a real problem: why would God deputize humans to do his dirty work of divine justice through war? If divine judgment must happen, then so be it, that's God's prerogative. However, from my perspective it should be lightning bolts from heaven, not uncle Jacob with a machete. I'm not fond of this plan at all. But the very fact that I am having this moral quandary is, for me, additional evidence for the existence of God. If God does not exist and we are simply products of time and chance caught in a meaningless existence, there should be no moral dilemma; conquest happens, the fittest survived, and if they used "God" to motivate their people to accomplish their agenda, what concern is it of mine? Instead of blustering angrily, Dawkins should be praising the Jews on the evolution of clever schemes of conquest for the sake of survival, and yet what happened "in the name of God" still appears wrong to him. It only feels wrong, because (to Tom Holland's point) Dawkins is more Christian than he knows!

All of this helps me to a extent. Still, despite all of these caveats and explanations, terrible atrocities were indeed committed in the name of the same God who Christians believe sent Jesus into the world. No amount of effort can sweep away the unease I feel when I think too long and hard about this. No one should kill babies or defenseless children and women. It is wrong for God to command it and then deputize his chosen people to carry it out. It is wrong by God's own standards. The Jewish Torah says to be kind to the stranger. Proverbs says to do good to those who are evil. Jesus says to love your enemies. The Apostle Paul says not to seek revenge. These passages of God-ordained slaughter contradict the better story, yet here they are, without even a hint of criticism, objection, or condemnation.

The narrative arc of the better story is full of ideas that—through Jesus, the ultimate hero of the story—allow us to embrace a life characterized by forgiveness, mercy, grace, and love. Ancient tribal warfare and the all-too-common brutal struggle to carve out a homeland is only one small but dark and troubling chapter in what is otherwise the most compelling story. If the norm of this grand story was the vengeful brutalizing of humans at the whim of an angry, unhinged God, then yes, the story should be thrown out. But that's not at the heart of this story—not even close.

End Notes:

[72] Richard Dawkins, *The God Delusion*, (New York: Bantam Books, 2006), 31.

Chapter 21

Does the Bible's support of hell ruin the better story?

Christianity is such an odd religion. The whole image is eternal suffering awaits anyone who questions God's infinite love. Believe or die. Thank you for all those options.
Bill Hicks

    A friend of mine sat on my couch with a glass of wine. We had been talking about what comes after death, according to the Christian story. He took a sip and said, "Why can't God listen to his own sermon on forgiveness? The concept of a permanent hell seems so unforgiving to me. That's why I am more of a reincarnation guy; you keep coming back with a fresh chance to learn and grow, a new chance to make better choices. That's a way better story! Hell is just too final for me to believe in."

My friend has a strong point. If the fiery furnace is the final destination for the majority of humanity, how is that in any way good? How does this fit with the character of God? This part of the story is so objectionable that virtually all newcomers to the faith I have interacted with reject it out of hand. "Believe the better story," I say as I talk about the deep love of God shaping our lives. But then, as the conversation shifts to life after death and the idea of hell works its way into the story, things begin to sound more sinister in the ears of those who would listen. It's like I'm saying, "Believe the better story—or else!"

Scaring the hell out of someone was a successful strategy for pushing people toward Christianity in generations past. Perhaps no greater example exists than America's Great Awakening of the mid-18th century. Its wildly successful conversion rate can be attributed mainly to a terrifying fear of an angry God and a scorching hell. The most famous example is the sermon, "Sinners in the Hands of an Angry God," delivered by New England preacher Jonathan Edwards on July 8, 1741. Here is just a snippet of it; the entire sermon reads similarly.

> The God that holds you over the pit of hell, much as one holds a spider, or some loathsome insect over the fire, abhors you, and is dreadfully provoked: his wrath towards you burns like fire; he looks upon you as worthy of nothing else, but to be cast into the fire; he is of purer eyes than to bear to have you in his sight; you are ten thousand times more abominable in his eyes, than the most hateful venomous serpent is in ours. You have offended him infinitely more than ever a stubborn rebel did his prince...he will only tread you under foot. And though he will know that you cannot bear the weight of omnipotence treading upon you, yet he will not regard that, but he will crush you

under his feet without mercy; he will crush out your blood, and make it fly, and it shall be sprinkled on his garments...It would be dreadful to suffer this fierceness and wrath of Almighty God one moment; but you must suffer it to all eternity. There will be no end to this exquisite horrible misery. When you look forward, you shall see a long forever, a boundless duration before you, which will swallow up your thoughts, and amaze your soul; and you will absolutely despair of ever having any deliverance, any end, any mitigation, any rest at all. You will know certainly that you must wear out long ages, millions of millions of ages, in wrestling and conflicting with this almighty merciless vengeance; and then when you have so done, when so many ages have actually been spent by you in this manner, you will know that all is but a point to what remains. So that your punishment will indeed be infinite.[73]

If we are talking about "better stories," this isn't it. One time, a gay friend of mine who was contemplating embracing the Christian faith became so thoroughly flummoxed by the notion of hell that he became speechless. Finally, after several failed attempts to address the subject, he raised his eyebrows, cocked his head, and gave me a look that said, "I hope you have a good answer about this one!" I had filled his head with visions of forgiveness, love, belonging, and purpose, and now at the end of months of beautiful conversations, it seemed like the message I had been sharing had turned sinister. Could God actually say, "You better believe my wonderful story of redemptive love, or else I'm going to torture you forever"?

I wasn't sure what I should say; but this is what tumbled out: "I believe that in the end, God will do what is good, right, and true. We as humans don't always know exactly what that might be, which is why we trust God. I am no hellfire and brimstone preacher, but I do know where they get their material from."

And that's the challenge before us. Edwards wasn't just making this stuff up as a clever trick to scare people into being good Christians. His sermon is crammed to the brim with Bible verse after Bible verse supporting his violent conclusions. Notions of hell do exist in the Bible. There are loads of places where God is not happy at all, and vengeance is very much on his mind.

So now what? For many, like it or not, hell is part of the story; it must be embraced. Somehow the fires of hell are a good thing, or at least a necessary thing. Comedian and armchair theologian Thor Ramsey brushes off criticisms against eternal punishment. God's redeeming love can only be truly appreciated if there is a hell:

> If Hell freezes over... the loss of eternal punishment as it is taught in the Bible will result in the shrinkage of God's attributes and, in the end, a smaller God. We will suffer the loss of the fear of God, the loss of a holy God, the loss of a just God, the loss of an extravagantly loving God, and the loss of God's wisdom on the cross. We can't afford to lose the attributes of God. Otherwise, we have a meaningless gospel... It's the difference between Jesus dying for you or just giving up His seat on the bus for you.[74]

Ramsey is not about to go along with this drifting tide of "envangellyfish," as he calls them—the Christians who believe, for example, that hell is only a metaphor, or a temporary holding tank that eventually dissolves into heavenly bliss for all, or shorthand for annihilationism (that the bad guys stop existing). To Ramsey, without a robust hell, all is lost; the entire Christian story is robbed of its power. Because the doctrine of hell is so central to him, Ramsey cracks jokes and quotes Bible verses throughout his book and makes his case that a punishing eternal hell is very real, very terrible, and to be avoided at all costs—through faith in Jesus.

The reality of hell lands like a gut punch to the stomach of my faith. I don't like a story that finishes in flames for so many. Who would? This doesn't connect to the longings of my heart at all. Is there any other way to understand hell that can avoid Edward's horror movie version while at the same time does not cheapen Jesus' sacrifice?

The better story is about bringing heaven to earth, not about escaping hell

With Jesus, the purpose of the church centred on bringing about God's kingdom on earth. Jesus' message to his disciples was that heaven was coming to earth: "Let us think of ways to motivate to acts of love and good works. And let us not neglect our meeting together, as some people do, but encourage one another, especially now that the day of his return is drawing near." (Hebrews 10:24-25)

The culmination of this message was that Jesus would come again and fully establish God's Kingdom on earth. He dropped a pretty clear hint at the end of the book of Revelation: "Yes, I am coming soon!" To which John replied with enthusiasm, "Amen! Come, Lord Jesus!" (Revelation 22:20)

The Apostle Peter was in complete agreement that Jesus was

coming back soon: "The end of the world is coming soon. Therefore be earnest and disciplined in your prayers" (I Peter 4:7).

Early Christians spent their time eagerly working to make the world a better place in preparation for the imminent return of Jesus. Jesus' prayer, "May your kingdom come, may your will be done on earth as it is in heaven," was taken very seriously.

Early believers spent their time joining God in preparation for heaven's glorious joining with earth. Even after the first generation of believers started dying off, the focus was still earthward—not heavenward. Paul comforted the believers who were wondering how death fit into the plan, now that people were dying in advance of the Lord's return. He told them that when Jesus came back, he would bring the departed with him to earth (I Thess 4:13-17).

There is no talk of heaven or hell or any afterlife. That's not the focus of the story. But as the centuries passed, Jesus still did not return! "Jesus is returning soon," as the answer to all of life's big questions started to feel worn.

Remarkably, the church grew in power to such a point that this religion, first perpetuated by Jewish fishermen, took over the Roman world! By AD 313, it had functionally become the state religion of the Roman Empire. So what now? Where was Jesus? Why didn't he come? Thoughts began to shift.

If heaven was not coming to earth, Christians reasoned, then earth needs to get to heaven. If God is not coming to us, we need to figure out how to get to God. Gradually, the purpose of the Christian life shifted to preparation for the afterlife. Within some strands of Christianity, heavily influenced by Gnosticism[75] in particular, the world became a deplorable place; anything material, including one's own body, became a trap, a jail, a place to escape. The problem was sin; heaven could not be obtained so long as sin existed in a person's life, so what could be done? Asceticism[76] was born as an effort to abolish sin. Verses like 1 John 2:15 became immensely popular: "Do not love the world nor the things it offers you, for when you love the world, you do not have the love of the Father in you."

People began to worry about the consequences of not being good enough to make it into heaven. Sin is hard to get rid of completely, and no evil would be allowed in heaven. From at least Pope Gregory (590-604) onward, sin and its abolition became the absolute focal point for most Christians. Attaining God's presence in heaven was the goal, and every Christian became responsible for eradicating his or her sins to accomplish this. Lists were created describing in blushing detail every imaginable sin and its corresponding penance required to purge the stain. Spiritual practices like confession, penance, the Eucharist, last rights, baptism, Lent, and memorizing the catechism became essential rungs on the ladder you had to climb to get to heaven. And as big organizations are wont to do, administrative authority was created to ensure Christians correctly jumped through every hoop. Priests became the certified agents through which people might achieve heavenly bliss. Fear and terror of death became convenient tools for spiritual leaders to make sure their flocks made the proper provisions for the afterlife. As the church bureaucracy grew, these provisions increasingly came at a cost. There was money to be made in the business of afterlife preparation. People will always pay for insurance, and no insurance was more valuable than making sure you spent eternity in the right place.

John Fisher recorded his observations as he sat by the death bed of King Henry VII on April 21, 1509: "The king died a good Christian death but his last days were far from peaceful. They involved confession, prayer, weeping and a dying man trying to bargain with God...." Fisher's account, which goes on for pages, is one of a man in agony, "not for the dread of death only, but for the dread of the judgment of almighty God." This upsetting piece of historical literature shows that Henry VII was panicked by what might happen to his soul after his death. In his terrified state, he left behind a vast sum of money with instructions for the church to say 10,000 masses for him. Surely, he thought, this extra effort would help secure his safe passage into heaven.[77]

To this day, for many Christians, the grand story of God does not culminate in a worthy king returning to heal the earth. Instead, it holds to a lesser story of how to placate an often-angry God and avoid the fires of hell. This tragic misfocus twists the story in a direction it was never meant to go.

The better story is that Jesus will return to make all things new. That is our hope and our focus. Standing at the gates of heaven and hell with a clipboard, taking roll call, has never been the goal or the point of the better story.

But what about those who do not work to bring heaven to earth? What about the wicked? What about the hell passages and the heavenly ones? All good questions, but not the primary questions.

If hell does exist, it is a prison locked from the inside

Most people, myself included, recoil at the notion of hell because we assume its inhabitants want to get out. Thanks to medieval artists influenced by the divergent version of the gospel outlined earlier, we envision hell's occupants as caged prisoners held against their will, and we see God as an uncaring prison guard who laughs at their misery. C.S. Lewis presents a much different understanding of hell than Jonathan Edwards does, one that I'm inclined to think is more accurate.

In Lewis's imaginative work *The Great Divorce*, the inhabitants of hell prefer it over heaven even though they are miserable. In his story, a bus filled with hell's occupants takes a trip to the fringes of heaven. The people of heaven try to convince the people of hell to give up their suffering and stay in heaven; surprisingly, none choose to stay! According to Lewis, all inhabitants of hell are self-absorbed. They are at the centre of their own ever-shrinking, ever-solitary, ever-suffering universe. They want themselves more than joy itself. When confronted, they lash out, blaming others for the mess they are in. Some are interested in God, but only as a means to an end. God is useful to better their kingdom of self or to get whatever they want. For others, heaven is seen as a place to become a shining star. In every case, when the people of hell realize that they cannot get what they want out of God and heaven, they become disgusted with it. "It's better to suffer in my kingdom than worship in God's," they all conclude. This was also Satan's choice, and the choice of every one of hell's occupants. As only Lewis can, he describes how the ghosts of hell continue to shrink back into themselves, getting smaller and smaller until they cannot even be seen. It is pure misery for them all, but they choose it. The doors of hell are locked from the inside.

Better stories care about justice

Whatever hell is, justice is the big idea behind it. The need for justice is something every human understands and accepts. No one shrinks back from justice being served on earth when a righteous judge slams his gavel down and delivers a verdict upon a guilty person. It is the right thing to do. It is the good thing to do. It is the better thing to do. Hell is the gavel of justice coming down upon the guilty. The more a person has been robbed and violated in this life without any recourse, the more open they tend to become to the idea of divine justice.

Our cultural context has a much bigger influence on our ideas of hell than many of us realize. A Rwandan man would likely welcome the idea of hell after witnessing his entire family and village slaughtered. It's more difficult in the West for some of us to accept the concept of stern divine justice when the greatest injustice we face is the slightly imperfect temperature of our Starbucks latte. We should be careful as we sit in the comfort of our easy chairs not to become appalled at a God who might be upset with an evil that we don't understand or experience. The only hope for many in our world is that a righteously angry God will one day lash out in perfect justice in favour of the downtrodden and oppressed. Pastor and author Tim Keller makes this point particularly well, using original thoughts from Yale theologian and Balkan war survivor Miroslav Volf:

The human impulse to make perpetrators of violence pay

for their crimes is almost an overwhelming one. It cannot possibly be overcome with platitudes like, "Now don't you see that violence won't solve anything?" If you have seen your home burned down and your relatives killed and raped, such talk is laughable—and it shows no real concern for justice. Yet victims of violence are drawn to go far beyond justice into the vengeance that says, "You put out one of my eyes, so I will put out both of yours." They are pulled inexorably into an endless cycle of vengeance, of strikes and counterstrikes nurtured and justified by the memory of terrible wrongs.

Can our passion for justice be honoured in a way that does not nurture our desire for vengeance? Volf says the best recourse for this is belief in the concept of God's divine justice. "If I don't believe there is a God who will eventually put all things right, I will take up the sword and be sucked into the endless vortex of retaliation. Only if I am sure that there is a God who will right all wrongs and settle all accounts perfectly do I have the power to refrain."[78]

Many questions remain about hell. Is it temporary? Will those that continually shrink into themselves eventually become non-existent? Is it possible for the fire of hell to have a purifying effect that ultimately results in the salvation of some or perhaps all of the damned? Those are interesting questions debated regularly among Christian scholars. For those of us living a daily life of faith, they are academic conversations—nothing more.

In summary, the gospel is found in the story of heaven redeeming earth, in "all things becoming new", as the Apostle Paul put it. The good news was never intended to be reduced to a fire insurance policy against an unwanted afterlife destination. In the grand scheme of cosmic justice, I believe the guilty will know who they are, and they won't object because they prefer themselves over God, no matter what the cost. Finally, whatever hell is, justice is at the centre of it. In Divine judgment, a more perfect version of our human justice system, we have a flawless, heavenly judge who will only carry out decisions that are good and right and true.

This perspective on hell removes terror and fear from the conversation. It reorients me to my role as one who works to prepare the earth for the coming king. It helps me value the need for justice in our world, and, most importantly, it eliminates hell as a bludgeoning stick that beats me back into my mortal cage.

End Notes:

73 See https://www.blueletterbible.org/Comm/edwards_jonathan/Sermons/Sinners.cfm

74 Thor Ramsey, *The Most Encouraging Book on Hell Ever* (Adelphi, Maryland: Cruciform Press, 2014), 31.

75 Gnosticism is the belief that human beings contain a piece of God (the highest good or a divine spark) within themselves, which has fallen from the immaterial world into the bodies of humans. All physical matter is subject to decay, rotting, and death. Those bodies and the material world, created by an inferior being, are therefore evil. See https://www.worldhistory.org/Gnosticism/

76 Asceticism is the practice of the denial of physical or psychological desires to attain a spiritual ideal or goal. See https://www.britannica.com/topic/asceticism

77 See https://www.tudorsociety.com/21-april-1509-the-death-of-henry-vii/

78 Timothy Keller, *The Reason for God* (New York: Penguin Books, 2009), 74-75.

Chapter 22

Do the Bible's prudish views on sex ruin the better story?

I recognize that for many, nothing I can say can counteract the Christian track record on sex and sexuality. Christians have been responsible for too much abuse, hypocrisy, and historical lunacy to offer a wise word worth listening to. If you close the book here and now, I understand completely. If you don't, I promise I won't try to make a bad situation worse!

When Christian views about sex were actually a good thing.

The big priority in Christianity when it comes to sexuality is faithfulness. The Christian vision of a successful marriage is for one man and one woman to join together for a lifetime.

Sexual relationships outside of this union are frowned upon. This fidelity would have been rare indeed in Greek and Roman times. In addition to his wife, who would bear his children, a man was culturally free to, and even expected to, sleep with concubines, mistresses, enslaved people, boys, and temple prostitutes. This culture of sexual promiscuity and power dynamics created a broken relational landscape fraught with sexual abuse, pain, and suffering. The Christian story confronted this broken landscape with a story of equality. From the lowliest slave to the emperor himself, all people were equally valued in God's eyes. The customary sexual advantage-taking that existed because of a person's status in society was no longer acceptable in the Christian story.

The only way this level of loving equality could be achieved in such a sexually broken society was through marital fidelity. This is why the author of Hebrews said, "Give honour to marriage, and remain faithful to one another in marriage" (Hebrews 13:4). It's why the Apostle Paul boldly declared the Christian vision of marriage equality when he said, "But because there is so much sexual immorality, each man should have his own wife, and each woman should have her own husband. The husband should fulfill his wife's sexual needs, and the wife should fulfill her husband's needs. The wife gives authority over her body to her husband, and the husband gives authority over his body to his wife. Do not deprive each other of sexual relations…" (1 Corinthians 7:2-5a).

These Scriptures were mind-bending, radical, culture-shattering statements. But the motivation behind them was not to ruin peoples freedom. Instead, they were a love-infused plan to help vulnerable people escape the abuses of inequality. In this light, Christianity's more restrictive perspectives on sex don't sound so bad. Today, especially in the wake of the "#Me Too" movement, we can clearly see that our situation in a post-Christian Western world does not rise much above ancient Rome and Greece. Has the sexual freedom we so aggressively fought for produced more equality, belonging, and care—or less? Maybe those early Christians were on to something.

You can't have it both ways

But isn't faithfulness to one person in such a singles-dominated, sex-saturated culture unreasonable? Sex columnist Dan Savage thinks so. When asked about long-term commitments, he said, "Yeah, absolutely we need to rethink love and commitment.... Monogamy is ridiculous; we aren't any good at it, we are not wired for it, it's not natural...we need to develop more realistic attitudes about sexual exclusivity." He believes sexual exclusivity is a recent phenomenon. Since the beginning of time, he says, men have never practiced monogamy. "Only in the 20th century, as male and female relationships became more egalitarian, did we shift to sexual exclusivity." According to Savage, this was a huge mistake: the better course would have been to open up the door for women to be more unrestrained sexually in their relationships rather than to close the door on sexual freedom for men. Savage insists that he is not against monogamy per se, just for a less exclusive version. "If you stay with the same person for 40 to 50 years and only cheat a few times, you are really good at monogamy," he says.[79]

Savage's thoughts are tempting, and the bleak statistics evidencing our inability to practice faithfulness give credence to his more open philosophy of monogamy. But can you cheat only a few times and still be monogamous? No, you cannot. Savage's casualizing of sex does not work. We have never been able to be as casual as we would like on this issue.

The yearning to belong exclusively to someone forever remains unchangingly desirable. The co-mingling of naked bodies is the loudest cry to belong, to "fit in" that the human has. To dismiss it as recreation, a hollow biological function, or something so common as food or sleep is to speak a lie to the deepest parts of the human soul. The unending stream of heartbroken people smashed to bits by betrayal is more than enough evidence for me that sex is a cry that goes far deeper than mere recreation.

Even the entertainment industry, which effortlessly splashes casual, meaningless sex in front of us, betrays a deep uneasiness with this narrative. Music, art, and movies constantly express in gripping terms the longing for belonging that only faithfulness provides, and the devastation we feel when our trust is betrayed.

A great example is the 2018 movie *Bohemian Rhapsody*, a biopic of Queen's legendary frontman Freddie Mercury. Freddie's deep love interest was Mary, but with the fame and riches that came with being on top of the rock n' roll world, he could not bring himself to commit exclusively to her.

"Your life will be difficult," Mary says to Freddie with genuine care when they finally part ways. "I love you, Mary, but..." was Freddie's all too familiar refrain to the only person who genuinely loved him. She had to let him go. Freddie seemed to want commitment, the foundation for lasting love, but he also wanted a bit of everything else, and you can't have both.

Freddie's ruthless disregard for musical convention and his radical commitment to creativity are the reason for his band's unprecedented success. He was an experimenter and a rule bender, to the benefit of music fans everywhere. Sadly, he applied these same attitudes to his sexual life. What was a blessing musically became a curse relationally. His excess destroyed his ability to belong. Once his ego was sufficiently big, it was only a matter of time before he distanced himself from those who cared about him the most—Mary, his band members, and his family. Freddie Mercury's free love perspective first enslaved him and then destroyed him. Without faithful love, there can be no belonging. Without integrity in relationships (not just sexual ones), a person becomes lost and, worse yet, truly alone. In the end, the movie sorrowfully portrays the despair that comes as Mercury's life spirals out of control. Is it any surprise that the lyrics to his most famous song repeat that soul-crushing phrase of ultimate despair—"nothing really matters"—over and over again? Deep down, Freddie knew there was a better path: faithfulness to Mary. Throughout the movie, he keeps trying to make his way back to her. But you can't belong to one person and a host of other people at the same time, no matter how much Dan Savage tries to make us think we can. In the end, as Freddy dies of AIDS, he leaves almost all of his wealth to Mary. The parting gift is a testimony to the high value of exclusive love, something Freddie intuitively desired but was unable to attain.

Let's stop pretending we know everything

Debra Hirsch, the author of *Redeeming Sex*, was sexually abused by men early and often into adulthood. She developed same-sex attraction, almost as a defense mechanism against predatory men. She became part of a communal lifestyle and shared her bed with men and women. Then she found Jesus and eventually stumbled into an ultra-conservative seminary with a strong desire to learn more about the Bible. As Hirsch recounts in her book, she was shocked to learn that people at the seminary might frown on her "freer" perspective on life and sex. She was puzzled when they turned down her request to have a male roommate in the seminary dorm room—it wasn't like that, she told the administrator; she wasn't even into men that way! Eventually, Hirsch would graduate from the seminary and marry a guy named Alan. Together they would become the dynamic and influential writer/speaker duo they are today. She goes to great pains in her book to convince her readers to stop pretending to know it all. Her primary message is that the world of black and white does not mesh well with the complexities of human sexuality.

Is this person gay? Is this person not? Is this person trans? Is this person not? Hirsch's message on our never-ending desire to categorize and label people is clear: "Stop it!" She has been gay, bi, and straight at different times for many different reasons. Hirsch even says, "It's okay to have intense same-sex attraction and not have to view oneself as gay."

"The gap between gay and straight is not often as clear for women as for men," she writes. "Perhaps this accounts for the rise in women who identify as bisexual."[80] Feelings and attractions ebb and flow; people are different; people change; we all make choices; life happens.

"Simple binary categories of homosexual and heterosexual are not really good enough," she continues. "They don't do the job, everyone has a story and not everyone fits neatly into those categories. Given that everyone's experience of sexuality is not only multifaceted but unique to their story, it's almost impossible to place a generic label on a whole group of people and think you've defined them... Anthropologist Jenell Williams Paris says, 'Try to define gay or straight, and the words begin to slip through our fingers.'"[81]

She goes on to confirm the complexity of human sexuality by quoting the American Psychological Association:

> There is no consensus among scientists about the exact reasons that an individual develops a homosexual, bisexual, gay, or lesbian orientation. Although much research has examined the possible genetic, hormonal, developmental, social, and cultural influences on sexual orientation, no findings have emerged that permit scientists to conclude that sexual orientation is determined by any particular factor or factors. Many think that nature and nurture both play complex roles.[82]

Her point is clear: whatever you think about human sexuality, there is an excellent chance you do not know it all. Christians would do well to dial back their certainty on these issues.

The importance of being pro-choice

Years ago, I watched a movie in which a hockey player was confronted by a girlfriend accusing him of cheating on her. He stares at her blankly while she gives him the business. When she's finished, he shrugs his shoulders and says, "I'm a hockey player; hockey players fornicate. It's what we do." Nothing could be different for this man. Monogamy was out of the question; it simply was not part of a hockey player's DNA. The woman would just have to deal with it. Is this true? Is the hockey fraternity destined to be forever cut adrift from the possibility of faithfulness?

One time an atheist friend of mine surprised me and came to one of our worship gatherings. I was delighted to see him but also a little bit concerned. On this Sunday, I had chosen to quote heavily from David Bentley Hart's book *Atheist Delusions*. Even though I was only using the historical part of the book to communicate how paganism had fallen prey to the better story of Christianity, I was concerned that something in the book, or even Hart's regrettable title, might put him off. So I reached out to him to make sure he was okay. We made plans for coffee.

Thankfully, he wasn't offended by the book's title or any perceived criticism of his atheism. He was put on edge by a more usual culprit. In my sermon, I criticized how we as a society had systematically reduced our freedom of choice, especially in human sexuality. I contested this bleak deterministic perspective, suggesting that it would not result in human flourishing.

In the coffee shop, my friend was emphatic that there is no choice when it comes to the complexities of human sexuality. Everyone is just whatever they are, and we have to accept that.

I gently pushed back. "Let's imagine that you wake up next to your wife in bed one morning, and suddenly you have this incontestable epiphany that you are no longer monogamous—it's just not in your DNA. The startling realization that you have been living a lie the whole time you have been married shocks you. What are you going to do? Are you going to lean over, kiss your beloved on the forehead and say, 'Sorry dear, I'm just not wired this way. I'm going to have to start exploring other women now?'"

He looked at me for a long time as he pondered his answer and said, "Correct. You have no choice."

But when choice is evacuated from the bedroom, belonging and responsibility are sacrificed to narcissism. Human sexuality is complex, to be sure, and in many situations, there are no easy answers for the right way forward. But "it is what it is" helps no one. We all have to make choices in life that go against our nature at some point.

For same-sex attracted people, it becomes immediately challenging to see how choice could even be a possibility. Without exception, all my many gay friends have confided in me at some point that they have wished they were not gay.

I agree that people's orientations are both settled and deep, and they cannot simply wish them away. Gay Christian activist Matthew Vines says that a person's orientation is both unchosen and fixed and that a same-sex attracted person can never be attracted to the opposite sex. He speaks passionately and convincingly from his own experience.[83] But his non-negotiable decree is not entirely accurate. Both Rosaria Butterfield and Debra Hirsch are living examples of the contrary.[84] So too is my friend, whom I will call Max. He is a same-sex attracted man who is a professional minister. He chose to marry a woman and raise a family. He chooses to manage his same-sex attraction within the context of his marriage. When he told me this, I immediately had a bunch of questions. How could this ever work? When I took him and his wife out to lunch, I got to hear their story.

Max was open about his same-sex attraction growing up, and his church met him with compassion and care. He assumed a celibate lifestyle must be his calling, so he busied himself serving within the church family. He identified first and foremost as a loved child of God. Yes, he struggled with same-sex attraction, but he did not want that issue as his primary identity. He was happy. He experienced a profound sense of belonging within the connectedness of a loving church family. Eventually, he became an executive pastor. After some time, one of the secretaries at the church developed a crush on Max. Naturally, he was oblivious. When one of his co-workers pointed out this woman's obvious care for him, he had no idea what to do.

"Take her out on a date, you goofball," he was told.

"Yeah, but why?... you know," Max replied.

"Don't worry about it—have fun."

Max asked her out, and she said yes. Max told her about his same-sex attraction from the beginning, and they agreed they would just be friends. Over time, they became best friends, but there wasn't any sexual attraction. Until one day, three years or so into their friendship, Max experienced, quite unexpectedly, and for the first time, opposite-sex attraction. It was only for this one particular woman, and undeniably the more significant attraction in his life was still men. Still, perhaps God was opening a window of opportunity? They cared for each other, loved each other, and made a good team. After much counsel, they got married. Their marriage has lasted so far and produced two children.

"Is it hard to love a man not naturally attracted to you?" I asked Max's wife as we finished up our lunch.

She thought for a moment. "Sometimes," she said. "Every woman wants to think that she is attractive to her husband, that my body might excite him, but we get on well enough. We have our good moments. We are happy," she concluded with a smile.

Their love is more about the daily companionship that comes from a committed relationship and raising a family together. Are they missing out on something? They seem identical to every middle-aged couple that's been married for a long time. Sexual desire is not always the first thing on the menu when it comes to committed, long-lasting love.

"And what about your same-sex attraction? I asked him.

"There are days when it's stronger and days when it's not as much, but we manage it. I'm happy, and I'm content with the life God has given me," he answered.

Our sexual proclivities, whatever they might be, run deep, and I do not want to minimize that. As a heterosexual, I recognize that my attraction to the opposite sex could hardly be considered a choice. I also do not want to suggest that Max's story become the story of every same-sex attracted person. When I ran Max's account by a couple of my gay friends, one said, "Well, good for Max, I'm happy for him—but just don't try to force that shit on me!"

The other was more skeptical of the arrangement. He had attempted to make a relationship work with a woman many years previous. The entire experiment ended in heartbreak, misunderstanding, and total failure. "Talk to me about him in a few years," he said. "I bet they won't be together anymore." He might be right.

Even still, I believe choice is a good and needful thing. We are not creatures destined to obey our natural instincts. We must never give up on the conviction that we always have a choice, whatever our situation.

Compassion is the most important factor

In Chapter 12, I shared the story of my friend Derrin. I concluded that chapter with the following sentence: *My entire friendship with Derrin and its attendant journey into faith would have never been possible had our church had a policy about gay people. The better story is the one that, at its core, demands a genuine love for other people regardless of the complexities of their sexual lives.*

I cannot underscore the importance of this final point enough. Christian people too often have become self-righteous, arrogant know-it-alls who, perhaps in their desire to please God or stay pure from the "wicked world," have set up barriers to loving, supporting, and caring for people who are not monogamous or heterosexual. This is a great tragedy.

I don't have policies or concrete answers for complex questions surrounding topics like gender dysphoria, divorce and remarriage, cohabitation, sexual orientation, gay marriage, masturbation, pornography, birth control, fertility treatments, and a hundred other sexual conundrums; but I do have the gospel story of self-sacrificing love that shapes how I interact with people of all kinds. This story, if I'm willing to listen to it, constantly pushes me towards deeper care for everyone, especially those most different from me.

End Notes:

[79] Dan Savage, See, https://www.youtube.com/watch?v=w8SOQEitsJI, *"Why Monogamy Is Ridiculous."*

[80] Debra Hirsch, *Redeeming Sex* (Downers Grove, IL: InterVarsity Press, 2015), 70.

[81] Ibid.,112.

[82] Ibid.,113.

[83] Mathew Vines, *God and the Gay Christian*, (Newark NJ: Audible, 2015), Chapter 2 55:09.

[84] Both of these popular Christian authors switched from homosexual relationships to heterosexual relationships at some point following their conversion to the faith.

Conclusion

Escaping the Mortal Cage

Life has a way of shaping the stories we believe. Sometimes life sticks the middle finger in the face of redemptive love. Understandably, there are times when the brutality of our lived experience convinces us that life outside the mortal cage is impossible. Such is the case with so many of my friends as I read and re-read their stories recounted in section one. Their lived experiences so often push me away from confidence in God. The bars around me strengthen, and there are times when I feel powerless to escape.

It is also true that some, like me, are naturally skeptical of supernatural realities. The wildly hopeful dreams of the Christian vision are just too much to stomach. Especially when they bump up against such formidable challenges to living faith as the reality of hell, prudish perspectives on sex, and those pesky genocide passages. All of these pressures combine to cage me in and snuff out the light of faith within me. "This is all there is," is the relentless refrain that crashes on me like waves on the ocean shore. The ghostly shade of ultimate meaninglessness whispers its darkness into my soul. But I resist it; as part of the fraternity of uneasy believers, I live in cautious rebellion against it. I am learning that despite all the challenges before me I can still slip the bars of my cage and embrace a vision of reality that has redeeming love at its centre. I can do this because I've received good help from the doubters. They've permitted me to wrestle, be unsure, and question my faith without fear.

With doubt as a friend rather than a foe, I've seen that the entire human race operates on faith. In this, we are all the same. Everyone's faith anchors itself in some overarching story, and as I've observed, some stories are better than others. One particular story that continues to linger in Western consciousness, even after its unofficial dismissal, is Christianity, from which many competing stories are poached. When it comes to connecting my life path to one of these grand narratives, the truest question I can ask myself is, "What do I long for?" These are the longings I should listen to.

Mystery promotes trust far more than certainty ever could. Great confidence is good if you want to sell something, but it's not the best companion for the humble walk of faith. I've become more cautious about embracing rigorous apologetics, realizing that an overzealous defense of the faith can miss the whole point of belief. I've had to overcome Biblical Attachment Disorder. Our Christian holy book is a valued treasure map, but it is emphatically not the treasure. Finally, the regular infusions of hope and purpose, all centred around the story of divine love, have undeniably changed my life for the better.

It has taken years for all my musings to settle into a cohesive whole that brought consistent comfort. Even now, the mortal cage is never very far away, and some days are better than others. But I'm not afraid of doubts like I used to be. I'm not as worried or depressed by my less-than-spectacular faith. I belong to the fraternity of uneasy believers, and in the company of such outstanding doubters, I manage to escape my mortal cage. I walk away from its stale, lifeless confinement into the beauty and wonder of creation. As the sun shines and the fresh ocean breezes blow, I embrace the deeper longings of my heart. My faith remains, my hope endures, and my love grows.

www.ingramcontent.com/pod-product-compliance
Lightning Source LLC
Chambersburg PA
CBHW042113100526
44587CB00025B/4041

THE GAUQUELIN EFFECT

A PROOF OF CELESTIAL INFLUENCE

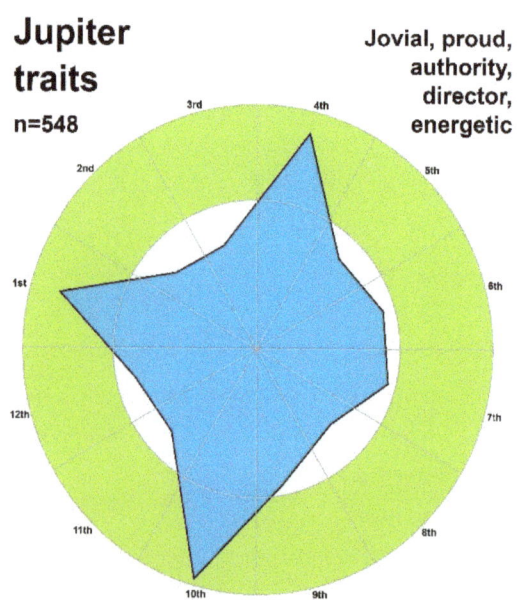

The character-traits of Jupiter

THE GAUQUELIN EFFECT

by

Nick Kollerstrom

M.A. Cantab., PhD, F.R.A.S.

A **New Alchemy Press** publication
www.newalchemypress.com
Copyright © 2023
Nicholas Kollerstrom
The author has asserted his moral right to be
identified as the author of this work.
Any part of this publication may be reproduced or utilized,
but kindly acknowledge the source
ISBN 978-1-7399994-6-9

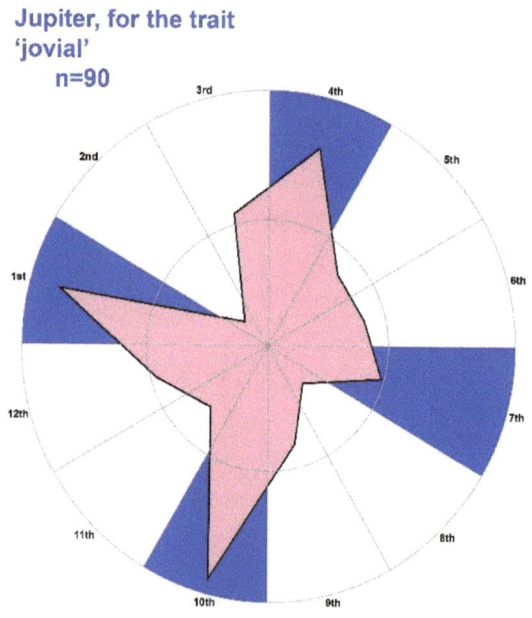

Figure: Is Jupiter jovial?

Thanks to the Urania Trust, for a grant; to Sven Raphael, Ray Murphy, Thierry Graff, Rudolf Smit, Derek Norcott and Graham Douglas; and to Fiona Bowring for cover design.

CONTENTS

Intro	by Rob Hand	
Foreword		1
Chapter 1	Looking at the data	12
Chapter 2	How Big was the effect?	27
Chapter 3	So Brief a hope	38
Chapter 4	Sceptics hit back	51
Chapter 5	Ertel: Did Michel cheat?	75
Chapter 6	French Skeptics see the Mars Effect	95
Chapter 7	A Search for 'proof'	112
Chapter 8	A 'Heredity' effect? Not really	133
Chapter 9	Character traits	140
Chapter 10	The Primary archetypes	146
Chapter 11	Venus found	165
Chapter 12	John Addey's dream	173
Chapter 13	Introvert / Extravert	182
Chapter 14	Synastry of Parisien couples	193
Conclusion		202

Introduction

Both those who are for and against astrology (in the broadest sense) as a serious field for study recognise the importance of Gauquelin's work. It is probably not putting it too strongly to say that everything hangs on it.

> Arthur Mather, Zetetic Scholar 1979

I would argue that the ground-breaking research of French statistician Michel Gauquelin provides us with compelling evidence for the existence of meaning in our world.

> Ray Grasse, The Waking Dream, Unlocking the symbolic language of our lives, 1996, p.266

For nearly forty years, contrary to what skeptics claimed, the Gauquelins had been right. They had found a replicable planetary connection that was also independently replicable by others.

> Dean et. al., Astrology Under Scrutiny, 2013, p.128.

The Gauquelins have no way of proving that they did not cheat

> George Abell, 'The Mars Effect', Psychology Today 16(7) 8-13.